The Coffee Break Guide to Self Publishing

THE STEP-BY-STEP GUIDE TO
SUCCESSFULLY WRITING, PUBLISHING,
AND PROMOTING YOUR OWN BOOKS

Amy Denim

Coffee Break Publishing
Denver, Colorado

Amy Denim/Coffee Break Publishing
www.coffeebreakpublishing.com

Book Layout ©2013 BookDesignTemplates.com

The Coffee Break Guide to Self Publishing/ Amy Denim. —1st ed.
ISBN 978-0990406044

Contents

Dedication

*For all the authors who are taking
the publishing world by storm.*

Acknowledgements

Phew, this book took me a long time and more work than I expected to complete. Holy research, Batman.

I wouldn't have finished without the encouragement of my awesome critique partners, Diane Whiddon and Sean Thomas. You all give great suggestions and make my writing better, whether it's non-fiction or romance. Thanks for making sure I see things from other perspectives and all the woo-woo.

I'm so glad for Kyle Hearn of Readited Editing. Hurray for commas!

Thanks to my family for believing that self-publishing is as real as traditional publishing, and encouraging me to do it the way I needed.

Big hugs to Romance Writers of America and Colorado Romance Writers for making me the knowledgeable and business savvy author I am today. How do writers make it without you?

Finally, thanks to all the authors and writers out there that ask me questions and want to learn about how to be successful in the publishing business. I learn as much from you as you do from me. Keep 'em coming.

If you want success, then don't rely on other people to do what YOU can do!

—Sasha Azevedo

Why Self Publish?

The publishing world, she is a changing. It used to be you could only get your stories and ideas to readers via the gatekeepers of the written word, agents, editors, and publishers. Writers had to slog through query letters and slush piles, enter contests or slip their manuscript under the bathroom door to get it read by anyone (Don't ever do that last one.). Even if you got a bite, it could still take years and complete rewrites until your original book is nothing like what you see on the shelf. You probably got very little say into the title of the book, the cover, and you definitely had to make changes to the actual story. But, hurray, you were a published author.

Now you could go on the fancy book tour, get the apartment in the city and the vacation home at the lake and take long leisurely strolls while working on the next book.

Or not. Because that's better fiction than any of us can write. We all know that 99.99% of authors are not rolling in the cookie dough. You may have gotten an advance, but it was probably only enough to live on for a couple of months at most. Not to mention waiting another year to earn out that advance and possibly see some royalties.

If, and that's a big 'if', you do get another contract with the publisher, they have now become your customer, not the reader, because you have to write what they want.

Not as glamorous as it looks on TV, is it?

Then came the age of self-publishing. It started out pretty rocky, with writers, fed up with New York, finagling a way to take a credit card and emailing their customers PDF files to be read on computers. But then, yippee, the e-book and the digital readers were born. The house that Jeff Bezoz built (aka Amazon) jumped on board as did Mark Coker (the creator of Smashwords) and made self-publishing available to anyone and everyone. However, the self-published books were poorly written, had never seen the light of an editor's red pen, and the cover...well, let's just say, oops. Self-publishing got a bad reputation as only for writers and manuscripts that weren't good enough to be published traditionally.

Luckily for us all, writers the likes of J.A. Konrath, Bob Mayer, Marie Force, Amanda Hocking, and Barbara Freethy, who are kick-ass at their craft, decided they wanted to have more control over their careers. Thank goodness.

Fast forward to today and writers have more power and control over the words, their careers, and the market than ever before. Is there still some crap out there? Sure there is, because not everybody takes the time to educate themselves like you are right now. Good on you.

So, why did I write a book about self-publishing? There were just too many good reasons not too.

Authors really, really want to see their books in the hands of readers. Sometimes that deep-seeded need can blind us. Someone such as a small niche publisher says they want to publish your book and whoopee, we jump at the chance. But is that really the right choice? Argh, I get so frustrated seeing some talented authors get taken advantage of by a small independent press who will never sell more than a few copies of the book. They get poor editing, cheesy covers and no marketing support. Plus, their books are way over priced so as to pay for the publishers production cost. That really irks me. To those of you who are looking to contract with a very small independent publisher, wait, just a minute. Hear me out.

What is that publisher going to do for you that you can do for yourself? Can you make as much or more self-publishing as the non-existent advance they aren't offering? Are you willing to sign a contract with them, give up the rights to your book, all because you feel like it will give you some legitimacy?

All I'm saying is be careful. Do some research on that particular publisher. Not all small independent presses are crapshoots. Sometimes it's a good idea to take a chance with one. In fact, I'm in favor of being a hybrid author, so all your books aren't in one basket. But, is it really worth it if your book is going to earn you $0.07 royalty checks.

I spoke at a lovely little conference in Colorado this year about social media and business plans for authors. Questions about publishing and self-publishing always come up in those kind of workshops and I'm happy to answer about my own journey, and what I know about getting books out into the world. Fun times. I could talk writing and the business all day long. So, why not write a book about it and make it available to everyone?

But where do I get my information?

My background is writing romance. When I first got into it I joined Romance Writers of America. Absolutely the best thing I ever did for my career. The romance genre and its writers are often looked down on by the rest of the world. I can't tell you how many times I, my friends, or other romance writers I know, are asked when we're going to write something real. Ugh. Because we're starting from the back of the pack in respect, romance writers must do everything they can to make sure they are ahead in the industry. The best way to prove it is through book sales.

Romance (the books, not the dating/anniversary/Valentine's schmooze) is more than a billion-dollar-a year-industry. In 2013, $1.08 billion dollars' worth of romance books were sold (US billions). That's about 20% of all book adult fiction book sales. Almost 40% of all e-book sales are romance, plus romance readers by 27 books a year on average. (The typical American admits to reading only five books a year.) Romance is approximately one-third larger than the entire inspirational book industry, and bigger still than the mystery novel genre and science fiction/fantasy genre markets combined. It's only outmatched by thrillers by just a smidge, and I'll bet some romantic suspense books like J.D. Robb's (aka Nora Roberts) were thrown into that category.

Romance writers are some of the savviest business women (mostly) in the publishing industry. We love to share our knowledge, hence the hundreds of conferences and workshops every year. When it comes to publishing, romance writers know their stuff.

If you don't write romance (maybe you should) that's okay. Because, like I said, we love to share our knowledge with other writers, and I want to share with you what I've learned over the past few years. Some of the ways I tell you to do things is my opinion on what's works best, based on my own self-publishing efforts and the knowledge I've accumulated learning how to do it myself. Are there other ways to get your book out there, absolutely, and if what I tell you to do doesn't work for say, your self-published math textbook, then let me know what you did and I'll see if I can add some new information to the next edition of the book.

And yes, there will be updated editions. Publishing is changing so fast these days, we all can hardly keep up, but this book should be good for a few years at least, and hopefully we get a few of your books up for sale in that time.

This book is for you and here's how to use it

This book is mostly for writers of fiction novels, but almost everything can also be applied to non-fiction books (like this one). This is maybe not the book for you if you're a free-lance article writer, unless of course you've been secretly writing the next great American novel in your basement for the past ten-years.

You'll see there are six main sections of the book. The nitty gritty of actually self-publishing isn't until section three on Pre-publication. But, don't skip those first two on doing your research and writing the book. Maybe you've been writing in your genre and you know your stuff (because you're probably a romance writer), but maybe there's something new or possibly forgotten information there for you. Give it a whirl, just to check to make sure all your bases are covered. I simply want you to have the best manuscript you can when you self publish it, so you can be successful.

Maybe you're a newer author and don't know that much about your genre, or maybe even what genre you're writing. You don't know what you don't know, right? Right. So please, take advantage of those first two sections to make sure your ducks are all in a pretty, little row before you skip to the pre-publication section. Because, just like those seasoned author who are looking for self-publishing advice,

I really want you to have the best manuscript you can when you self publish it, so you can be successful.

I love seeing authors become successful because of my business books. It makes me feel like I've contributed something to the world. Please, take advantage of my scholar/artisan personality and learn all that you can about being a really great self-published author.

CHAPTER ONE

Do Your Research

So you want to write a book

Are you sure? Because it's a lot of work. Can you write every day? 1000, 2500, 5000 words a day? Is there time in your schedule to write five to seven days a week? When do you want this book of yours to be released?

What genre is your book? Is there a subgenre? Do you know the guidelines (like word count, never kill the puppy?) for that genre? Does your book even fit into a genre? Have you read other books in that genre?

Are you a plotter or a pantser? Do you even know what that means?

What kind of story structure will your book follow? Three Act Structure? Hero's journey? Save the Cat?

If you have a positive answer for all those questions than you are ready to write a book. Yay! If you said no, I'm not stopping you from writing - you are.

I'm not being mean, I'm being a realist. Do you really want to write a book, or not?

Say yes, and then do it!

All right, I've either scared you away, or given you a pep talk. (Or I made you mad. Feel free to say "Screw you, Amy!" and go write the book your own way. I hope you do.)

Are you ready for reality check number two?

I've heard something similar to this 'rule of ten' dozens of times over the years. The numbers are not actual statistics, but anecdotal evidence from authors all over the world.

The rule of ten.

In traditional publishing -
One in ten people say they have a great idea for a book.
One in ten of those will actually start.
One in ten of those will finish the book
One in ten of those will send the book to editors and agents
One in ten of those will get their manuscript requested
One in ten of those will sign with an agent
One in ten of those will sell a book to a publishing house
One in ten of those will sell enough books to cover their advance.
One in ten of those will become a bestseller.

Yikes, so that must be part of why self-publishing has become such a booming industry.

So let's try our rule of ten again starting after finishing the book.

One in ten of those will get their book critiqued and edited.

One in ten of those will get a professional book cover

One in ten of those will sell more than 100 copies of their book

One in ten of those will sell more than 1000

One in ten of those will sell more than 100,000

One in ten of those will hit a bestsellers list.

Are you the one?

(Hint: Say yes.)

Great. Let's get started.

So you wrote a book

Some things you might have missed

If you've already published, this might help you with the next book, so don't skip this section.

You might already know a lot of this, but I learn something new every day. Hopefully you'll get a few new tips and tricks.

Maybe you even think, ugh, I already know all this. But, give some of this writing section a chance, if we're both lucky you'll get something new to add to your knowledge base.

Don't go it alone

For the most part, writers are a friendly, if introverted bunch. If they've spent any amount of time in publishing, they've gotten over the ego and into the ready-to-help-other-authors phase. Yes, that's right, other authors want to help you become an author.

We aren't all really competing for readers, most people read more than one book in their lifetime, and those superfan genre readers are voracious enough to read everyone's books. By helping you, other authors are really doing themselves a favor by promoting their own books via your own.

Case in point. Fifty Shades of Grey. Whether you read it or not, loved it or not, it brought a whole slew of new readers into the romance genre and opened the doors for thousands of erotic romance writers to cash in on the writing they'd been doing for years, or gave an opportunity for new writers to get some action. That book did wonders for a lot of careers besides EL James.

Does Ms. James bemoan when a new BDSM ingénue/billionaire erotic romance hits the stores? No way. Did all the writers of romance sigh and wonder where all their sales were going when Fifty hit the shelves. Not for a second, because, their sales weren't going anywhere but up the charts.

Okay, now that you're convinced other writers are your friends, where can you find your new writerly friends?

Join your genre's national writing organization. There are lots of them out there. Try Romance Writers of America, Sisters in Crime, Science Fiction and Fantasy Writers of America, American Society of Journalists and Authors, Society of Children's Book Writers and Illustrators, Alliance of Independent Authors, Novelists, Inc., or a plethora of others. Then find out if they have a local chapter.

No national? Join a local writing organization. I live in Colorado and there are more local writers' organizations that I can count. Rocky Mountain Fiction Writers, Northern Colorado Writers, Pikes Peak Writers, Colorado Romance Writers, Crested Butte Writers, Castle

Rock Writers, Lighthouse Writers, and a dozen I'm sure I missed. I bet your state has quite a few too. Google it, you'll find them.

No local group, because you live in Inner Assrackistan or Upper Lunarsurfacegolia? Join some online. Facebook has plenty of writers groups. Have you tried LinkedIn? People are frothing at the mouth to share writing tips and tricks with you there. Also, check out Yahoo groups. There are several specifically for self-published authors.

Now that you're in a writing group, pay attention, ask questions, and glean everything you can about the publishing industry. The better educated you are about craft, writer's life, publishing, marketing, and all the other things writers like to talk about, the better your books will sell, because you'll know what you're doing.

Educate yourself

The biggest mistake I see new-to-the-business authors do is to be uneducated about publishing. Gah, it drives me nuts when a newbie writer signs a contract with a tiny publishing house that isn't going to do a thing for them just because they said they wanted to publish his/her books. (Note: I don't think there's anything wrong with small publishing houses, there is something wrong with seven cent royalty checks.) There are plenty of self-published authors out there I just want to take by the shoulders and shake because of the fool mistakes they're making.

Joining a professional writers group is the first step to getting educated, but there's so much more you can do so you look professional and present a professional product to the world.

First off - read. Yeah, that's right. Writers read, a lot. Read in your genre, read outside of your genre, read craft books (not the Martha Stewart kind, the James Scott Bell, Michael Hague, Donald Maass kind), read marketing books, read how-to books (like this one), but read.

Take classes. Continuing education courses rock. I love me some online classes, and I bet your local writing organization has some great workshops. Go to them.

Go to conferences. I know they are expensive, but they are sooooo worth it. Not just because you can take an entire semester's worth of classes from industry experts but also for the networking. After your long day of taking notes and wiping away the tears from your eyes during the inspirational keynote speaker's address, hit the bar. Don't sip your Sazerac in the corner, join groups of other authors, and bring your business cards.

Go to the library. Libraries often have all kinds of great events for writers. They don't just have the research books and Internet access you want. They love authors there (for what is a library without books?). Look for programs about publishing, writing, public speaking, social media, and books in your genre.

Whatever you do, however you do it, get educated, because this is a multi-katrillion dollar business and you don't want miss out on sales and discoverability because you didn't know what you were doing.

Know your Genre

Hopefully I've convinced you get some knowledge into your head about publishing, and when you do that, I hope you'll learn about your genre, because nothing is worse than a book that's really a mystery parading as a cookbook.

So, you've decided to write a romance, or mystery, or action adventure, or literary collection of short stories, or a cook book, or a how-to book, or your memoirs, or, or, or.

Awesome. You've identified your genre.

But, what if you haven't? Time to do some research.

How do you know what genre your book fits into?

Try finding about ten other books that you think people who would read those books might also like yours. If most of them are all in the same genre, there you go. That's you.

You need to know the guidelines before you write (or before you edit that finished novel that's been under your bed for ten years.)

You wouldn't go out and drive a car without learning some basics about cars and the rules of the road first, would you? Okay, maybe you would (or did), but you probably weren't very good at it, and other people didn't want to be on the road with you.

It's the same in writing. You need to know some basic rules or guidelines before you get out into traffic. I hate the word rule, because a rule to one person is a ridiculous barrier to greatness for another. However, every genre has some guidelines you should understand.

Can you break these 'rules'? Sure. Break one or maybe two, and you could have some fresh hot fiction on your hands or the next great self-help book. Break a whole slew of them and you're going to get horrible reviews and no one will want to buy the book.

It's a great idea to know the rules before you break them.

But some of the greatest artists in history were great because they were innovators and broke all the rules.

Take Picasso. Nobody had ever seen anything like what he created and it certainly didn't follow any rules.

Oh, but wait...

Picasso studied art for years. He painted way more works that you can count practicing the styles and the techniques of the masters. Only when he felt he really understood the rules of art and portraiture did he know how to break them to create something new and innovative.

One of the great advantages of self-publishing is that we have the freedom to write something new and out of the box. Publishers have a lot of justification to do when they buy a book from an author. They need to know that it will sell and so they stay safe.

You might have the next great novel, but if it doesn't fit into the publisher's prescribed genres and money making antecedents, they aren't going to go for it.

As your own publisher you can write anything you want. Well, not anything, but you can push the limits.

How can you learn about these guidelines?

Read in your genre

Yep. This is the best way to learn how to write a good book. Read lots and lots of other books. Just because you have a great love story to tell doesn't mean you can write a romance. Same goes if something scary happened in your childhood and horror novels. So, unless you're writing a book in your very favorite genre that you've been reading for twenty years, it's time to head on down to the bookstore, or hit Amazon.

Two or three books isn't enough. I'm talking hundreds... for real. Get reading.

Research sub-genres

Every genre has a lot of subgenres. The more you can narrow your idea the easier it will be to find fans for your book.

The easiest way to describe sub-genres is with cook books. There are cook books for all kinds of different ethnic foods, like Mexican, Italian, Polish, etc. Then within that there's even more sub-genres. If you've got a Mexican food cookbook is it from a region of Mexico, say Oaxaca, or is it Tex-Mex? Maybe you're from Colorado and it's

Mountain Mex. You could narrow it even more and have Home-style Oaxacan food from the grill. Yummy.

Fiction has subgenres like this too.

It's important to stay on top of subgenre changes. I recently read an article about a book shopper who came upon a sign at their local bookstore with a whole new section especially for Dark Fantasy. Good news for the dark fantasy writers because it means their small subgenre is about to go to the big house.

The same thing happened to me a few years ago while perusing my local Barnes & Noble, and I ran into a whole wall of Young Adult Paranormal Romance. Thank you very much Stephanie Meyer.

Now, I'm not saying chase trends. That will kill your career, but keep up with the times because it will help you decide what to write next.

Word count is one of the easiest guidelines to figure out. Most single-title books are 75-120,000 words, so it's easy to start there. Each genre has its own word count. Fantasy novels tend to be longer and category romance is quite a bit shorter.

The easiest way to figure out how many words you should shoot for is to pick those ten books and see how many pages they have, then multiply by 250-350. A single-title book is about 400 pages, multiplied by 250 words is 100,000 words.

Trends and norms are important for you to figure out for your genre. For example, for years, romance novels were about 200 pages long, and that all important love scene was always always always on page 176. If you were writing romance 20 years ago, you needed to follow that guideline if you had a hope of getting published. Times change and so do trends and norms in genres. (Now you can have a love scene on page one if it is an important element to your story.)

High fantasy/action adventure novels might have the "Ice Monster Prologue." (Check out Dan Wells story structure videos on YouTube for more information about that.)

When you do your research here, you need to use the most recent books you can get your hands on. Plus, you should join the national organizations for your genre, like Romance Writers of America, Science Fiction and Fantasy Writers or the plethora of other organizations. The good ones will have plenty of articles, classes, and workshops that will help you stay abreast of the norms for publishing.

Wanna get really down and dirty to study your genre and subgenre? Do a competitive analysis. The Coffee Break Guide to Business Plans for Writers has a template to do exactly that. Head on over to www.coffeebreakpublishing.com/books/resources to download the template for free.

To Agent or not to Agent

One of the draws of self-publishing is that you get to keep a whole lot more of the money your book makes. The royalties are higher and you don't have to give 15% to your agent.

But, should you?

Agents can be a great ally in your publishing career. It's their job to stay up to date on the industry, which allows them to guide you, give you advice, and keep you on track to success.

What can an agent do for you?

Some agents will critique your work and help you edit your book so it's the best it can be.

A few agencies have set up a self-publishing arm to their business and have already found cover artists, editors, proofreaders, formatters and publicists to work with you.

They can help sell other rights to your book. Think your book is going to become a movie? You'll need an agent to sell the movie rights. Are you hoping that your book gets picked up by a traditional publisher? You'll need an agent if you're selling it to any of the Big Six. The most common rights for self-pubbers to sell is foreign rights. Your book is translated into dozens of other languages and sold around the world. Sweet, but you need an agent for that.

Most agents don't represent self-published authors unless they are already well-established, selling strong, or have been traditionally published. So, if you think you want to have an agent start doing your research now on who represents self-pubbed authors. You'll have to query, just like a traditionally published author. Make sure you are keeping track of your sales numbers so you have a good idea of how well you are selling. Once you have a few books out and have the numbers to back you, start querying.

If you do decide to send your work off to an agent, again, do your research. They all have websites and will tell you right on them what genres they are looking for and what they will and won't represent. Don't waste your time by sending your erotica to an agent who only represents Christian Inspirational non-fiction.

Where can you find the right agents? Try AgentQuery.com. Writer's Digest has a guide to literary agents where they showcase new agents (who are young and hungry and are actively looking for clients). The Association of Author Representatives, Inc has a website too. If you joined one of those organizations for writers I told you to, many of them have information about agents specifically seeking manuscripts in specific genres.

Money

How much money can I make self-publishing?

I'll be very honest here. Don't quit your day job, yet.

You're probably not going to make enough money to provide a living. But you might be able to supplement your income enough to help pay the bills.

Purely anecdotally, I've heard that most self-published genre fiction authors with at least three books out make around $300-500 a month. I'm not saying you will make this much money. How well written your books are makes all the difference. No matter how many books your have out, if they are poorly written, you still won't sell more than a few. Yeah, even if you have a great cover.

Study the craft, get critique partners or beta readers and do everything you can to write a great book.

Then be smart about publishing. You're already ahead of the game by picking up this book and educating yourself about self-publishing. Good job.

The more books you have available, the more money you'll make. Seems like a no-brainer, but there's more to it than that.

One book out and you'll sell a few for a couple of months.

Three books seems to be the magic number to establish a foothold into your genre. People buy one, they like it, they come back for more. Ten books available should get you a pretty steady income stream.

Several well-known self-published authors suggest that you hit the ground running and publish five books all at the same time. If you can have a little patience and get a bunch of books written, edited, formatted and get pretty covers on them before you hit publish you've got a better shot at making some real money than publishing one book a year for five years.

But, don't wait too long to push that publish button either. If you're a slow writer and can only do one book a year, you might miss the self-publishing boat all together if you wait until you have five books ready to go.

Slow writers can make it too. If you can only write one full-length novel a year, could you add a shorter novella into your schedule? Novellas and short related stories are a great way to keep your fans coming back for more in between releases. If you're used to writing 100,000 word books it won't be that hard to add another 25,000 into your schedule. You can do it!

A big part of the how-much-money-can-I-make equation is book pricing and royalties. I suggest you join some self-publishing groups, the easiest ones to find are online, try Facebook and Yahoo groups. Most self-pubbers are happy to share their experiences and knowledge including pricing strategy. Smashwords does a yearly report every year for the RT Convention (Romantic Times Magazine) with all kinds of information that self-published authors will find useful. The 2014 report has everything from what price points sold the best to how word-count relates to sales. Check out their blog at www.blog.smashwords.com.

I recommend doing that competitive analysis we talked about earlier to figure out what the best price is for your book. According to my own research, I price my romance books between $2.99 and $5.99 USD, with $3.99 seeming to be the sweet spot for now. That can and will probably change within a year, so make sure you check.

Amazon has a fun new tool that I have no idea how it works, that will tell you what they think the best price for you books are based on their own sales information. It's worth a try.

Once you've determined the price for your books, the next step in the equation is royalty rate. Depending on where you sell your book and what price you sell it for will determine the royalty rate. For example - Amazon offers a royalty of 70% for books priced $2.99 to $9.99 USD. Although, they have a small delivery fee for e-books with 70% royalties. Check out the terms and conditions of each book sellers for other fees they may charge so you aren't surprised looking at your first royalty statement.

A book listed for $3.99 will earn $2.79 in royalties.

The next step in figuring out how many books you can sell. This one is quite a bit harder because there isn't any information out there, on how many books self-published authors sell. Most niche books don't sell a whole lot more than about 200 books, ever. Genre fiction, with mystery and romance at the top of the bestsellers lists, can sell that and much more in a month. This is where those self-published author groups can help you.

If you think you can sell 100 books at $3.99 with 70% royalties you'll make approximately $279.

Here's the whole equation with the example information.

100 x (3.99 x .7) = 279.

Because there isn't a lot of information available on how much self-published authors it's always great when you can find a reliable source. The romance author Brenda Hiatt offers exactly that. Several times a year she produces her *Show Me the Money* report where both traditional and self-published authors submit their sales and earning information to her, which she publishes keeping the authors anonymous, of course. The information is only for romance authors and publishers, but if that's not your genre, it will give fiction writers a little bit of an idea. But, keep in mind, romance is the biggest fiction seller, so skew your numbers down.

Find the report at http://brendahiatt.com/show-me-the-money/indie-earnings/

How much will it cost me to self-publish?

One million dollars!

Kidding. Sort of.

You can actually self-publish absolutely free, if you really must (but, I hope you don't have to).

Do you know a whole lot about writing and the writing craft?

Are you an MS Word expert?

Do you know how to use Photoshop, InDesign, Scrivener, Calibre and other specialty publishing software at a professional level?

Are you best friends with a professional book editor who owes you a lot of big favors?

Well, then you can publish for free.

If not, here are the things you might need to spend money on.

Editing is the most expensive part of self-publishing. There are three levels of book editing, developmental, copy, and proof. It's expensive, but worth it. More on this in the Pre-publication chapter.

Most editors charge by the page or by the word. As an example Writer's Digest offers all three levels of editing for manuscripts over fifty pages. The price ranges from $4/page for developmental or line edits and $2/page for proof editing. In my experience this is a middle of the road price. There are plenty of editors who charge a whole lot more, but they mostly have a lot of professional experience. The higher priced editors often work for traditional or small press publishing houses and freelance edit on the side.

Only you can decide how much you can afford to spend on an editor. If you really can't afford one, make friends with other writers and exchange services until you can afford one.

After editing the next biggest cost in self-publishing is the cover. Yes, you could do it yourself, but I don't recommend it. More on this in the Pre-publication chapter.

An original cover, designed especially for your book, with exclusive rights to the art on it will probably cost you at least $500.

That art exclusivity is pricey, and can cost even more if you commission the work or the photo shoot.

There are more options though.

For around $200 you can still get a custom cover where the artist will use stock photography images to create your cover.

Don't have that much money? Try pre-made covers. Most run around $40-80 and the designers will sometimes make minor changes, like font and font colors. There are a lot of very talented cover artists with whole catalogs of pre-made covers, but there are a lot of hacks too. Do that competitive analysis and choose wisely.

Formatting is one of the services you can learn to do on your own and probably still look professional. If you know quite a bit about using MS Word you can create your own design template. When you upload to some of the book sellers, like Amazon they convert it into the appropriate file for you. Voila, free.

But, formatting issues can make you absolutely crying into a tub of ice cream and guzzling a bottle of wine crazypants. So, you might want to pay for someone else to format your book and create all the formats, like pdf, mobi, epub and others for you.

You can even pay someone to upload your book to the book sellers and distributors sites if you happen to already be a gazillionaire. Otherwise, sit your butt down at the computer and do it yourself.

The other cost associated with your book will all be post publishing, and include things like marketing. I'll talk more about that in the Post Publication section.

I really recommend doing a budget for your books. Don't go into the whole thing blindly hoping you'll come out the other end a self-made millionaire. I know a really great book that can help you with budgets and all the other parts of running a self-published book career. It's called The Coffee Break Guide to Business Plans for Writers by Amy Denim. (Yes, that's me!)

When you're looking at all these expenses of getting your book published think of them all in terms of break-even. How many books do you have to sell to break-even on that cost?

If your editing is $500, and you've got a $3.99 book, you'll have to sell 180 books to cover the cost. If your cover cost you $125, you'll have to sell 45 books.

If your formatting cost you $75, you'll have to sell 27 books.

Add all those books together and you're looking at 252 books to break even. Be realistic, can you do that, and how long do you think it will take you?

You'll feel a lot better about spending that $700 if you've given yourself a year to make it back, and you'll be pleasantly surprised if it takes less than that.

CHAPTER TWO

Write the book

Butt in the chair

How much time can you dedicate to writing?

I know you have a full-time job, six kids, a farm to run, a sick grandmother, attend school part time, and are battling depression, but I fully believe that you still have time to write a book.

Is it going to be easy? No. If it was, everyone would do it. To get your book done and published, you're going to have to make it a priority.

It helps immensely if you can get the support of your friends and family. You don't have to tell them what kind of book you're writing if you don't want to, but tell them you're writing a book. Then ask them for help.

Start posting on Facebook or Twitter and find writing buddies there. Tell your friends and family to ask you about your writing progress. They will think you're cool just for trying to write a book (and later you can make them all buy it.)

The "I have a family" excuse

Mom, can dad feed the anklebiters dinner a couple, three times a week so you can have an hour to write? Or how about you declare cereal night once a week. Teach those kids some independence and let them get dinner on their own while you lock yourself in the office/den/bedroom/basement/laundry room and write.

Dad, can you ask mom to take the fam to the zoo/museum/aquarium once a month so you can have a whole day to write? (You might have to promise a fancy date night in exchange. Just sayin'.)

Is it worth it to get a babysitter a couple times a month to watch the kids while you zip over to the library or the coffee shop to write for a few hours? (Tip: The answer is yes.)

I know you're exhausted when they kids finally go down for a nap, but could you get some relaxation out of jumping into the world inside your head instead of the bed?

Keep a notebook or tablet with you and in those five or ten minutes you're waiting to pick up the kids to take them to soccer, get a few sentences written. Or, how about at soccer practice? There's an hour you could get some writing in while still smiling and waving to the kids.

Will you always get your words in while locking the kids in the TV room for an hour? No. Kids bleed, and puke, and pee, and hit their sisters, all of which will interrupt your writing time. But, training your kids now that sometimes mommy or daddy need some time to do the things they think are fun too and talk to them about what you're doing. I bet your kids will become your greatest supporters. (Mine will even occasionally make me a grilled cheese sandwich when I'm on deadline.)

When all else fails, I recommend reading the blog at http://peanutbutteronthekeyboard.com/.

The "I'm not a very fast writer" excuse.

We all wish we wrote faster than we do.

I believe that writing is a muscle like all those chiseled ones we see on the covers of romance novels. You have to work it out every day to make it strong. The more you write, the more you will be able to write.

Whenever I take a writing sabbatical/vacation, the day I get back to writing is always a sludge through molasses for my brain. On a good day I can write about 1400 words and hour for a couple of hours in a row. On a long day I'll write around 600 words an hour for five or six hours. But that first day back? It will take me all day to write 300 words.

The next day maybe 500, then eventually I get that writing muscle back in shape and get back to the big word counts.

Perfectionism can be your enemy. I know a writer that consistently writes about 500 words a day. It takes her all day and when they are done, they are beautiful and perfect. Her editor loves her. But she, her editor and her publishing house all wish she could write more than one book a year. The thing holding her back is perfectionism. She deals with it by writing every single day, because she can't afford to lose even a days' worth of words at that rate. If that's you, I'm sorry. I don't write that way. I puke the words onto the page and then go back and fix them. Sometimes they are pretty good to start out with and I don't have that much to fix. I can't fix a blank page.

If you're the slow writer, try writing without your mental editor for a day. Write whatever, even if you know it's total slop as it's hitting the page. You might be surprised what kind of gems you find.

For you slow writers, I recommend trying NaNoWriMo. Every November is National Novel Writing Month. One month to write a 50,000 word manuscript. A million people do it every year. Everyone doesn't always complete it, but hey, at least you'll get a few more words on the page than in a normal month.

If you aren't actually the perfectionist slow writer and want to increase your writing output, try Candace Havens Fast Draft class. She'll get you to write and edit a whole book in a month! www.candacehavens.com/index.php/workshops/

The "I have a full time job" excuse.

Write when you're not at work. Really. A full-time job means forty hours a week, right? Okay, so you're a lawyer and working a hundred and forty hours a week. There's still twenty-eight hours left. You know you weren't really sleeping that much anyway.

Seriously, you might have to give up some of your other free time activities to write instead. Remember what we said about making it a priority.

Try writing instead of watching TV. Skip a couple hours of surfing the Internet. Can you miss an hour of sleep every night? Get up a half an hour earlier, lay out your clothes for the next day, eat your breakfast in the car, so you have an hour to write in the morning.

Speaking of the car. I bet you have some sort of a commute. No, don't physically write while you're in the car, but there is software that can type when you speak. Give it a try. http://www.nuance.com/dragon/index.htm

Same goes for when you're working out. Although if you're the indoor treadmill type, set up one of those laptop trays on your equipment and write then.

I know Saturday or Sunday is your only day to sleep in, but set that alarm (maybe not as early as on a workday) and you can even write in bed if you want.

Keep a notebook or tablet with you and whenever you're waiting for dinner, a meeting, your flight (and you better be writing on that flight too - uninterrupted writing time!) get out your work-in-progress, and write a few lines. I, honest to god, know a multi-published, New York Times, multi-million dollar book contracts author who wrote whole books exactly like that.

The "I have to wait for my muse to inspire me" excuse

No. You don't. Just write.

Okay, that was a bit harsh. But, that is the oldest excuse in the unwritten book. Inspiration is all around you. If you can't find your muse, she wasn't the right girl for you anyway. But honestly, try taking five minutes before you sit down to write to think about what you want to work on today and what you want to accomplish. Close your eyes and visualize yourself typing if you have no other option. Tap into that big ole brain of yours and get those words on the page.

The "I'm a great procrastinator and would rather do the laundry than write" excuse.

I feel ya. Me too.

Turn off the Internet - get that software that will turn it off for you. www.freedom.com. Then write. No, don't get up to get a writing snack. No, no, don't call your friend to work on your plot. No, no, no, don't clean your office in hopes that it will make you more productive.

The dishes and the laundry and the vacuuming can wait. And for goodness sake, hide your cell phone. Sit in the chair and write.

The "My special someone is sick and dying in the hospital" excuse

This one is hard to call an excuse. I am very sincerely sorry for the pain and suffering you and your loved one are going through right now. It's really hard to write in times of severe stress. But, wouldn't it be nice to have an escape where you can funnel your fears, desperation, hopes, and prayers.

A very good friend of mine did exactly that when her husband was in the hospital fighting for his life. She spent the hours waiting at his bedside, waiting for doctors, waiting for sleep, turning her heartache into the monsters in her book. Guess what? In the end her husband recovered and the monsters were defeated by true love.

The "I'm the depressive artist type" excuse.

Yeah, me too. No, for real. I've struggled with depression since high school. It's hard to write when you are having a hard time talking yourself into being alive. But something that makes me feel better is, like above, having an escape. For all those right-brained creative people who are stifled in a suit and tie world, not having the chance to let your inner unicorn out to roam and eat rainbows is horrible and depressing. Find a way to be creative, like writing. It will help.

You can also siphon all those deep dark demons onto the page. It will help you, your therapist, and a whole host of others who suffer to know they aren't alone. Write. It will help.

Challenges

A few challenges that have helped me write more are the 100 words a day, #1K1Hr, NaNoWriMo, and the Book in a Year.

The 100 words a day challenge is exactly that. Challenge yourself to write 100 words a day (maybe for a hundred days). It's really not very many. A couple of paragraphs at most. But what the challenge does is gets your writing. Two things will happen when you take up this banner. Rarely will you only write a hundred words. Once you get going a hundred will turn into two, three, and a thousand. Even on the days you struggle and get stuck at ninety-nine words, at least you wrote. That's ninety-nine more words than you had before. What this exercise will really do for you is train you to write. Remember that writing muscle I told you about? We're here to pump (clap) you up!

#1K1hr is a hashtag on Twitter where writers can virtually meet up and challenge each other to write 1000 words in an hour. At the end of each hour you all report back on how many words you got and no matter your word count, congratulate each other. I get more words written in a day when I hop on #1K1Hr than any other time. Try it out, and look for me at @AmyDenim. I'd love to write with you.

NaNoWriMo is the acronym and fond nickname of the National Novel Writing Month. A cool organization called The Office of Light and Letters get people together online and in person to work on writing their novels. The goal is to write a 50,000 word novel in November. They have handy dandy word trackers, inspirational emails and a whole host of merchandise to keep you writing. If it's not November you can also join Camp Nano in the spring and summer to write a book of any length spurred on by cabin mates from around the world. Find them at www.NaNoWriMo.com.

If you make it through the hundred words a day challenge you're ready for the next one. Book in a Year (BIY). Again, self-explanatory. Challenge yourself to write one fully completed book this year. To make it a little more fun, my local writing group passes around a signup sheet and we pay to enter the challenge. We sign up for BIY with the title and genre of our book and put in five dollars. Whenever we get our "The End" we send the last page to the leader of the challenge to show we finished. Then every January those who actually finished the book get their names in the hat, and one lucky writer wins the cash. The chance at an extra hundred bucks sure motivates me to write a little more.

No matter your excuse for why you aren't writing somewhere is the answer. You have to search it out and find what works for you.

Where to put your words

You're ready to sit down and write your book. So you find a comfy chair at Starbucks, start up the laptop and open...

There are many programs that will help you write your manuscript. Some are designed especially for writers. Take a minute and investigate before you start that new document. You might find something that helps you get more work done.

The good old standby is, of course, Microsoft Word. Honestly, I use this about seventy-five percent of the time. It can get frustrating when you don't know all the ins and outs of formatting and that stupid autocorrect thing keeps changing your character's name from Jules to jewels. But it's pretty easy to open and just start writing.

If you decide to use Word, I'd recommend getting a template for your books. It will make formatting a whole lot easier when you get to that step. I got one from http://www.bookdesigntemplates.com and I love it. Joel Friedlander is the book design (and self-publishing) guru, so I trust him. See more about templates in the formatting section.

If you don't have word, OpenOffice has a program that is similar and is free. www.openoffice.org/

The next best loved writing software you should check out is Scrivener. This weird, but geeky cool dude, designed this software specifically for writers. There's a bit of a learning curve, and I recommend doing the tutorial at the beginning and checking out YouTube for videos, but once you get the hang of it, you'll like it. My favorite part is the corkboard feature. It's like having a giant bulletin board in your rough draft. The cost is $40, and there is a 30 day trial version you can try out to see if you like it. If you 'win' NaNoWriMo one of the prizes is a 50% discount for the program. That's how I got it. It's also available on Amazon or you can get the free trial and other tutorials at www.literatureandlatte.com

I'm using it to write this book, right now.

There are so many others out there it could be a whole book (that I am not writing!), but here are a few more suggestions for you to check out.

I preface the following with the caveat that I have never used any of these programs, but I thought they all looked cool when I was doing the research for this section.

Zen Writer is for those of you that get easily distracted. It even comes with soothing music to lull you into writing. There's a demo version and the software is under $20 to buy. Beenokle, the creator maintains a Tumblr blog with tips, tricks and updates. Plus, he says right on there that if you REALLY can't afford to buy ZenWriter to email him. Find his software at www.beenokle.com

Writer's Cafe was designed by a writer and looks pretty cool. It has a free trial, cost $40, but offers a $10 discount for full time students. www.writerscafe.co.uk/buy

Storyist has a word processor, story development tools and a project manager. It cost $59 and is only available for Mac and IOS. http://storyist.com/index.html

Page Four is by the same guy who did SmartEdit, which I do use and like. There is a trial version so you can test it out first and if you decide to buy it's $39. It's only available for Windows. www.softwareforwriting.com/pagefour

All of the following programs are free! Although, some have premium upgrades with more features or ask for a tip or donation with download.

Ywriter www.spacejock.com/yWriter5 is a great alternative to Scrivener, that many authors swear by, but only available for Windows.

Plume Creator www.plume-creator.eu is out there too (and don't be mad Mac peeps) and is also only available for Windows and oddly, Ubuntu.

If you're easily distracted, you might try Focus Writer. www.gottcode.org/focuswriter/ Guess what? It's available for Windows, Mac, and even Linux.

LitLift www.litlift.com/ is an online writing program and writer's community.

Once you've got some words on the page, whichever program you choose, for God's sake back it up! I can't tell you how many tears have been shed over lost words and crashed computers with whole manuscripts on them. Please, please don't let that happen to you. Back up, back up, back up.

DropBox is free for the first ten MBs and readily available anytime you have an internet connection.

SugarSync has a $99 yearly fee but will automatically back up any file you ask it to anytime you close or save the file. Again you need Internet access.

OneDrive and iCloud are sort of like a hard drive in the sky. Any PC with Windows comes with OneDrive or you can get one by creating a Microsoft account. If you've got a Mac, an iPad or and iPhone you already have access to the iCloud. Again, you need Internet access.

Flash drives are those cute little sticks that plug into your computers USB port and can hold an amazing amount of data. Big bonuses are that you don't need internet access and you can carry in your pocket. But don't lose it!

External Hard drives are bigger versions of Flash drives. They make them now with a capacity of a terabyte these days, which would be a ridiculous amount of books. Apple fans might want to look into getting the cool Time Capsule.

Email when all else fails, email a copy of your manuscript to yourself.

Other Handy Dandy programs and apps

There are a lot of other programs and apps out there to help you be the best writer you can. Don't go crazy downloading a crapload of stuff that you won't ever use, because, hey, you're just procrastinating the actual writing. But check out a few of these that might be useful.

For notes and research -

Scrivener has a great section for importing research, pictures and websites right into your project so it's there at your fingertips if you're using it to write anyway.

OneNote is installed already on most new PCs, but if it's not on yours it's a free download. I like the notebooks feature. I imagine it as a giant virtual Trapper Keeper.

Evernote is the favorite of a lot of writers for saving notes and clippings from the internet and it's free too.

Name Dice is my ultimate favorite app. I can't tell you how many of my characters' names came from this fun little iOS app.

Feedback

I know you're a kick-ass writer now, but you still need constructive criticism on your work. Don't shake your head. Yes, you do. I do, New York Times bestselling authors do, you do, everyone does. Feedback can help keep you from publishing rookie mistakes like clichés, the dream sequence opening and too many adverbs.

Critique is hard, so grow a thick skin now, like rhino mixed with Transformers mixed with Adamantium thick. Then get in a critique group.

It took me a while to grow my skin. I literally laid in bed for two days after my first serious critique. But then I pulled myself up, made some changes to my baby and sent it back out. That's right, it's your baby. You pour your heart and soul into your writing, if you're serious about writing, and then someone tells you your main characters isn't relatable and isn't empathetic, even though you specifically wrote in relatability and empathy for them. Ouch.

It's okay to cry a little, grumble, scream to the world (in the privacy of your own home, not publicly) that they are completely wrong. As long as you can pull yourself together later and make the revisions.

I'm not gonna lie, sometimes it is hard to find the right group with the right people. You need someone who is going to stick with it. That's the biggest frustration for most writers. You find a great group, with intuitive partners, who submit something for review once every three years. Blech.

You also need someone who is truly going to give you constructive criticism. They can't be too nice and say you're writing is great, but they can't be too mean and rip everything and you to shreds. You need critiques partners who understand your vision, will work with your voice and will tell you straight when something isn't working.

The number one truth I know about critique groups is they are great at identifying there is something wrong with your manuscript, but they very rarely know what's wrong. These partners look at your book and one person may be flat out stupid about what they think the problem is, two people have a problem and you can possibly ignore them, but when a whole group gives you some similar problems you know you have some work to do.

If you get a lot of conflicting feedback on a story point or a section of the book where one person tells you your dialog isn't working and someone else says you need more internalization and another person says they didn't understand your character's motivation, there is something wrong, but it might not be any of those things. You'll have to evaluate your own writing then and figure out what's missing or needs changing, but know that something does.

I recommend trying to find partners in your genre so they understand what you're writing about at a specific level, but any serious writers will do as long as you and they are willing. If you're writing romance and you join a group with Sci-fi, mystery and action-adventure writers they may say you need more guns and explosions where a group of other romance writers might know you are missing one of the twelve steps of intimacy.

Where can you find critique partners? Start with your local writing group. If they don't have anything running, hit the Internet. Those online writing groups I told you to join will be a great place to look for a critique partner. Just ask, because I bet there will be someone else online that needs a critique partner too.

Another great place to find serious critique partners is in writing classes and workshops.

There are a few websites that are specifically geared toward matching up critique partners. Try Ladies Who Critique www.ladieswhocritique.com/ (sorry guys), How About We CP http://howaboutwecp.tumblr.com/ (open to all genders), Critique Circle www.critiquecircle.com and CP Seek www.cpseek.com.

Critique partners are great because they understand writing, hopefully. But readers can give you great feedback too. If you have someone read your book when it's (mostly) done, but they aren't giving you writing advice, but strictly story advice, then they are a beta reader. They might not know you're hero, on his hero's journey is missing the gathering of allies section of the story, but they'll tell you they think he needs to have some friends help him prepare for battle in chapter ten. Reader feedback can be invaluable.

Where can you find beta readers? Social media is great for this. Try Facebook, some of your friends and family might like to help you by reading your book and giving you feedback. Superfans of certain genres like romance and mystery tend to hang out on Twitter and would love to be involved in your process. Try Goodreads too. The Writer's Cafe and Absolute Write each have a whole thread on their forums just for finding beta readers.

Note that there is a difference between a Beta reader and a paid critique. Beta readers usually aren't paid with anything more than love and a copy of the book when it comes out (or go crazy and buy them lunch or put a gift card in a thank you letter and mail it to them). A paid critique is just that. If you decide to pay someone for a critique be sure you check their credentials and see if they have the background and experience reading and critiquing what you write. A lot of paid critiquers are disguised at Beta readers, so just understand what you're getting before you pay for anything.

If you decide to go the Beta reader route, I'd suggest a questionnaire with specific information on the feedback you need. There's one available on my website at www.CoffeeBreakPublishing.com.

Remember that no matter how you get your feedback, it's still your story, your book, and you get to decide what happens in the end. Take or leave the critiques you receive and make an educated response on whether to change your work on not. But, you'll have a better book for having someone else read it before you publish it and your feedback comes in the form of one star reviews.

Editing

You need to do your own revisions before you think about sending your manuscript off to an editor. Don't make the rookie mistake of submitting a rough draft.

Whether you revise as you go or once you've finished your first draft they key to knowing when you're done is that you are really sick of your own book. Sounds funny, but it's true. You'll hate your book when you're done, but your readers will love it.

I suggest at least three rounds of edits.

1. Some people like to edit as they go, re-reading paragraphs, pages or chapters as they go. But don't get stuck in the revision cycle. One round of that is enough. Even if you revise as you go, I still suggest a once over of the whole manuscript. When you've finished the first draft, read through the whole thing on your computer and edit as you go. This is the perfect time to do mass find and replace of your garbage words, like just, really, and good. This is the round of edits where it's great to have a critique partner or group to help you with story and writing revisions. If you happen to be one of those crazy people who hand writes your first draft, you can do your first round of edits as you type it up.

2. After you've done your online edits print that sucker out. Highlighter and red pen in hand, read through the whole thing again, and make a lot of notes. Seeing your words in a different format will help you find all kinds of typos, misused words and other fun errors. You might even want to change the font before you print it out.

3. Make all your changes from the first two rounds and then print your manuscript out one more time (sorry trees). Now,

read it out loud. It may feel slightly awkward to read those sexy scenes to your cat, but I promise you'll find all kinds of things to change. When you stumble over a sentence look at your cadence, word choice or if you've echoed the same word fourteen times in the last three paragraphs. Make notes on your manuscript again and then go back and edit one more time.

There are so many books, classes, and workshops on editing and revising your work. I recommend two that I took, love and added to my own personal editing bible.

Check out Angela James's Before You Hit Send, http://nicemommy-evileditor.com/before-you-hit-send/. (That's where I learned to do the apostrophe s for possessives even when the name ends in an s, as in James.) This is a month long course that will make sure you don't look like a newbie.

If you're up for something more intensive that will change your writer for the better forever, sign up for Margie Lawson's writing courses. www.margielawson.com. Margie's EDITS system and her Master Immersion courses will give you fiction authors the keys to writing like a New York Times bestselling author (or even better.)

Some self-editing software programs out there can help. They all have paid versions that have all the whizzers and zoomers.

Pro Writing Aid http://prowritingaid.com/ has a free version where you can cut and paste your writing and it will give you some detailed analysis like overused words, clichés, passive voice, and more.

Autocrit has a free wizard (not like Harry or Hermione at all) that will catch some errors, but you're limited to 500 words at a time and can only submit three times a day before you have to pay. If you're diligent and check the writing you do each day, this is perfect, but it won't work for you if you're doing a big master edit. If you really like what it does and you're writing a lot you can buy a subscription.

For absolutely free try Edit Minion. It's not very complex and you can't paste too much at a time, but it's got some good reports to utilize.

If you want something you can use for long section of text and that you can use forever, you might consider buying some editing software.

I was lucky and got in on the Beta of SmartEdit. It has since been upgraded, and now cost $59. But, if you can scrape together the money you'll find it useful. You can download a trial version to see if you find it useful too. www.smart-edit.com.

Serenity Editor cost $55/$75 depending on whether you want the Word add in or not. They also have a free trial. www.serenity-software.com.

Style Writer has a free 14-day trial, and you could edit a whole book in that amount of time. www.stylewriter-usa.com.

Now that you're book is in the best shape you can get it into, it's ready for an editor.

Avoid those one-star reviews that are more about your typos than your story by getting your book professionally edited. Yeah, it will cost some money, but you'll make more money in the long run.

Don't shake your head right here and say you can't afford it. I couldn't either when I first started out, but you need to find a way to have somebody look at it before you publish. Your sister or your grandpa isn't the right person (unless they're a professional editor). If you really can't afford one, ask your local librarian if she might help you. Find an editor who is just starting out and ask if you can get on a payment plan. Swap services. Bake them cookies. Don't assume you can make the book good enough. Please.

Developmental editing is to help you make the story, a story, or the book cohesive. They look at premise, plot, structure, pacing, characters, dialog, and marketability. Critique partners/groups, beta readers, and contests can help you do this if you don't want to pay a developmental editor.

Copy editing or line editing is someone going through your work, line by line and suggesting advice on sentence structure and flow, redundancies, inconsistencies, and may include grammar, punctuation and word usage.

Proof editing looks specifically for grammar, punctuation, word usage errors and typos. You may not need a separate proof editor if you have a copy editor.

You may not need all three rounds of editing. If you've used a critique group or beta readers, you may not need the developmental editing. But, if no one but your mom and your dog have seen your work, it might help. A lot of self-published author go with a copy editor. It's more intensive than a proof read and will catch a lot of the same errors. At a minimum you need to have someone proofread. Not your mom, either.

A read proofreader and editor has had professional training or years of experience in the industry. They'll make you use the Oxford comma for clarity. They'll know when to use who or whom and when it just sounds silly. They know the difference between a hyphen, a dash, an en-dash, and an em-dash. Do you?

Hopefully I convinced you to find and use a professional editor for your books. Now you have to find one. But where?

Start with that writing group I told you to join. Specifically ask other authors who they used and how they liked the experience. Get recommendations.

If you didn't join a group yet, A. Go join a group, and B. Google is your friend.

Seriously, type fiction book editing or non-fiction book editing, or whatever you write and a whole slew of results will pop up. I suggest starting with the links that take you to authors' blogs with recommendations. Then pick a few, check out their website, prices, and testimonials.

CHAPTER THREE

Pre-publication

You finished your manuscript. Yay!

You might think the next step is to upload it to Amazon and push publish. Umm, not so much. You've got some work to do first.

Your Platform

Before we even begin to talk about the steps to getting your manuscript ready for publication, we need to talk about getting you, the author ready.

And no, I don't mean a make-over to get ready for your release day party. Sorry.

You've got to have a platform.

Wait, what's a platform?

I don't mean the kind that Ms. America pageant contestants have that include harsher punishments for parole violators, Stan...and world peace.

For authors, a platform is the where and how you interact with fans and potential readers.

I hope you've already started building your platform and if you have, awesome dude. Check through this list and make sure you've hit all the biggest and best places.

If you haven't, it's okay. Not great, but okay. We'll start now.

I've got a whole book on this called The Coffee Break Guide to Social Media for Writers. If you need more than just the minimum I'm presenting here, check it out.

Let's start with the absolute basics.

Do you have a website? Well, you need one. This is your home base. No matter what else happens, this is where people can find you and your books forever and ever. If I can't talk you into doing anything else, please have a website.

If you're starting from absolute ground zero and don't have any money to spend on a website, design, or designer, go over to www.wordpress.com. Sign up and in just a few minutes you can have a free website.

Use your name and maybe the word author in the URL. For example, www.amydenim.wordpress.com. When you do the free option you'll have to have the dot wordpress dot com in your URL, but I'm okay with that for now. Once you've got a little money to spend you can upgrade to a wordpress.org site, with hosting and everything. And when you've got a little more money, hire a web designer. You don't want your website to look amateurish, do you?

Your pretty new WordPress website comes with a built in blog. Blogging is a great way to get your name out there. Can you blog about your writing at least once a week? Great. If you shook your head and got the hives, then use that blog to announce your new releases.

Why should you be on social media? Discoverability.

People these days expect celebrities (and yes, now that you're an author, you're a celebrity) to be accessible. Facebook and Twitter are the best ones to start out with.

Get yourself a Facebook fan page and a Twitter account. Use your author name. You want everything to be branded; same picture, same profile, same name. Then get on those platforms and make friends. Notice I didn't say get on those platforms and promote your book. Can you do a little self-promotion? Sure. But, if all you do is say buy my book all day long, no one will want to be your friend, and even more, no one will listen when you say, "buy my book."

Social media is a place to be social. Talk about your writing, talk about your inspirations, talk about your cat. People like to see things they can relate to. So, relate to them. Then every once in a while you can tell them about your book and give them the link to check it out.

I suggest a rule of three on social media.

On Facebook, I recommend you have both a profile and a page. It's hard to be social when you only have a page, but when you do your promo posts be sure you're directing people to your page.

From your profile page on Facebook, scroll through your newsfeed and comment on at least three things. You can like as much as you want, but it isn't a real interaction.

Then post three things, a picture or a video, a question, or an anecdote. Your question or anecdote can be accompanied by a link to something else like an interesting article.

When you're done being social, do the last of your three things. Go out and make three new friends. Facebook is great at suggesting people you might know, but if you don't have any good suggestions, try joining a group and making some friends there.

Don't forget to post in similar fashion to your Facebook page too.

On Twitter, scroll through the feed and find three people to reply to, then share three tweets of your own in the same fashion as on Facebook with pictures, questions and super short anecdotes with links. Then go find three new Tweeters to follow.

Don't go crazy

There are a million billion other social media networks you can join. Don't try to do them all, you'll get social media brain fry. Also, don't feel like you need to be on for hours a day. I think you can do all your online networking in the span of a coffee break or two. The key is to find the social media platform that you actually like being on and then use it well.

In our crazy online world today, it may seem insane that we can even still meet people face-to-face. But in person, events are a great way to create a strong fan base.

Even as a debut author, with only one book to your name, you can do personal appearances. Check with your local libraries and book stores to see if they have any author events that you can join. Most libraries love local authors. We all know libraries are underfunded, so donate your book, or if your library doesn't take donations, ask them to buy it. Not all libraries can purchase self-published books, but certain distributors, like Smashwords and have programs for libraries to purchase e-books from them for their collections. Oh yeah, libraries have e-books now too.

Libraries also can't afford to pay all those big New York Times bestselling authors to come and speak, so, why don't you offer to do a program at the library for free?

If you've got a local brick and mortar book store, support the heck out of them. They'll return the favor. Most independent bookstores have some sort of author events and are happy to carry some self-published books. Go meet the owner and/or manager, bring them some cookies, bookmarks, and see how you all can support each other.

Lots of town have some sort of book fairs every year. See if you can get a table, booth, or be a special guest.

Writing or Special Interest Groups are always looking for guest speakers. You wrote a book, so you're an expert on something. Give a talk about it.

Talks and workshops are not only a great way to promote your book and find new fans, but they can also be a supplemental source of income for you. Many groups will either pay their speakers or offer a small honorarium to their guests and it doesn't hurt to ask if you can sell books after the event. If you can't, at least do a giveaway or two for the audience, and be sure to ask the winners for a review.

A Business Plan

The Coffee Break Guide to Business Plans

Have you thought about putting together a business plan? But, oh, it's such a long and complicated process. Ugh. Why bother, when you could spend your valuable time writing. But, wait, what's this? A guide to help authors write a business plan on coffee breaks?

Okay, so I find when things get boring and staid that some humor and creativity makes it all much more fun. And let's admit that a traditional business plan is anything but fun. But having one can be an important part of taking control of your writing career. To get you started I've created a quick and easy set of questions that hit all the main parts of a plan and it really should only take you about a coffee break to complete it.

Put your thinking cap/top hat/beanie with the helicopter rotor/tiara on. It's time to think about what you really want from your writing career.

These questions are to get you started thinking about your goals, but don't go crazy and spend hours making lists and/or daydreaming about your success as a writer, I want you to do these on a coffee break.

I call this the Coffee Break Business Plan. This is all about basic goals, which you can expand on to create a full-blown business plan, so spend only a few minutes thinking about each of these questions. Write a couple of sentences to answer them or make yourself a nice bullet-point list. If you'd like a template to print out to help you with this exercise, you can download one at

www.coffeebreakpublishing.com/Books/Resources.

Grab a cup of coffee and a pen

Write down the answers to these questions.

How many books do you plan to write? In what genre?

What's your projected word count?

When will you finish each project? Or, how much time will you need to complete each project? (Don't forget to build in time for critiques, beta readers, editing, and all those other activities... besides actually writing the book.)

How will you publish these books? Traditionally, self-published, a hybrid approach?

If you're self-publishing, what services will you need and how much will you spend on those?

Who is your competition? Who else writes books like yours?

How will you sell and market your books?

How much money will it cost you to publish and market? What services might you pay for to help you do that?

How much money do you plan to make, and when will you see that revenue?

When do you plan to achieve these goals?

What resources do you need (such as a budget template, word count tracker, a reference book about business plans) to complete your plan?

When can you review your goals to see what you've accomplished and what you need to revise?

What rewards can you set up for yourself to say "Job well done!"?

There you go. You just created a basic business plan. For real. Laminate that sucker and put it up big and pretty in front of your computer. Every time you sit down to write, take a look and focus on writing to achieve those goals. If the IRS comes knocking, you can wave it in their faces.

Choosing where and how to publish your book

Are you going to write an e-book, a print book, or both? What about an audio book? With self-publishing, you can do any or all you choose.

E-books are where most of the action is in self-publishing. In the computer age, people want to be able to buy a book and start reading it with-in a few minutes, all without leaving their homes. You want to make your book available digitally.

If digital is such a big deal, why do you want your book in print? Maybe you don't. I'm not saying you must. But, don't you want to hold it in your hands, rub the cover across your cheek, and smell the pages?

There's nothing like the rush of holding your own book in your hands.

There are still people out there that want to feel that book in their hands too. Think about your market, your readers. Are they Millennials that can't look up from their phones or are they Baby Boomers who have a hard time reading the menu at a restaurant without extending their arms? Older readers are going to expect print books.

If you plan to do any personal appearances, you might want print books to sign, and they are great for promotional activities.

The audio book market is really growing. Again, in the digital age your readers can download or stream your book and listen on their commute. All without having three pounds worth of CDs.

The more formats you have available, the more readers you can reach. You won't sell as many print or audio books, but does it really matter if you've reached a few more rabid fans?

Might as well do them all.

Where are you going to make and sell your books?

I have a few suggestions for you.

Where to sell your books

You should sell your book digitally, but you can also sell in print, audio, and foreign translations as well. There are plenty of a lot places to sell your books, especially online. Let's talk about e-book sales first.

You really should sell your e-book at each of the five biggest e-tailers.

Remember, this guide is not legal or financial advice and should not be relied on as such. Unless otherwise noted, all references to amounts in dollars are to US Dollars. Publishing changes from day to day and it's entirely possible any and all of the publishers could change their royalty rates and payments. You can find the current royalty rates and other information related to payments on their respective websites.

Amazon:

KDP, CreateSpace and ACX - You'll do probably 90% of your sales here, so set this one up and publish here first. They recently introduced the pre-order program for self-publishers. Be sure to sign up for their Author Central and their Amazon Affiliate programs too. Readers can get your books on the Kindle, but also the app is available to download.

KPD pays 35% royalties for books priced less than $2.99 and more than $9.99. Books from $2.99 to $9.99 earn 70% royalties minus a delivery fee based on file size, except in certain foreign stores which only pay 35% unless your book is enrolled in KDP Select. They pay royalties approximately two months after the end of the month in which you sold a book. For example, if you sell books in January, you'll get paid at the end of March.

Create Space is Amazon's print company. There's more information below in the print sales section.

ACX pays 40% on books distributed exclusively through them (which includes on Audible, Amazon and iBooks), and 25% if you don't choose the exclusive distribution deal. However, if your book is purchased with credits through Audible's member program the royalty is calculated by how much money is in the member fund that month. You won't know how much that is until you get your royalty statement, but it's usually around $14.95.

They also pay approximately two months after the end of the month.

Apple: iBooks

To upload to Apple yourself, you'll need a Mac, or know and/or pay someone with a Mac, because their self-publishing app is only available for the Mac (you can't even get it on your iPad or iPhone - frowny face). You can sign up for an account and check your sales on a PC.

Apple also has the Apple Affiliate program that you can sign up for at PerformanceHorizonGroup.com. Apple pays 70% royalties approximately 45 days after the month ends. They also say their payment threshold is $150 before payment, but anecdotally, a lot of authors say they have been paid without meeting that amount.

Barnes & Noble

To sell your books on B&N you'll use NookPress. You can sign up for their affiliate program at Linkshare.com. Get an invitation through the NookPress helpdesk.

Nook offers two royalty levels based on list price: With a list price between $2.99 and $9.99 royalties are 65%. With a list price below $2.98 or greater than $10.00 (but not more than $199.99 and not less than $0.99) royalties are just 40%. They also pay approximately two months after the end of the month.

Kobo

This company was one of the first on the scene in digital self-pubbing with their site Kobo Writing Life, and are now one of the biggest in the world with over 4 million titles in 68 languages in 190 countries.

They're a Canadian company, and so, they're just really nice. They aren't as big in the US, but they basically own Canada, and are big in the UK, Australia and New Zealand. Because the company is Canadian, French books and French translations sell great here.

They also have a pre-order program. For bonus points, they have a great affinity with independent brick and mortar book stores and show it with their partnership with the American Booksellers Association, which means thousands of independent bookstores can put Kobo e-books for sale through their own Web sites. Yay for the indie books store and yay for helping indie authors with discoverability. Kobo also sponsors author events at independent bookstores. Check into that if you've got a great local that you want to support.

Kobo also does their affiliate program through Linkshare.com.

Kobo offers 70% of the list price on books priced $2.99 and higher with no cap. Royalties are 45% for books priced from $0.99 and $2.98. And, super bonus for when you're ready to do some promo, authors can offer their e-books for free. Their one downside is they only pay twice a year unless you're selling a whole lot of books.

Google

The Google Play store sells books. Did you know? Soon enough everyone will. Get your books up there. The program is called Google Books Partner Program. Like Apple, Google supports enhanced e-books (EEBs) with embedded audio and video.

You might want to price your book slightly higher here because they'll automatically discount it, and Amazon will price match. It's the really the only one on the Android platform. Plus, you know, they're Google. They're going to take over the world. Be there when they do.

Google Play Partners is their affiliate program. IT's a little difficult to find Google's royalty rate. We (the collective indie community) think it's 52%.

Book-a-Million (BAM)

Soon you'll be able to add Books-a-Million (BAM) to that list. Keep checking in at www.diy.bampublish.com

OmniLit & All Romance e-books (ARe)

If you write romance, you definitely want your book(s) on ARe. These two sister companies can also distribute to Apple iBooks if you don't want to use Smashwords and don't have a Mac.

They don't do file conversion, so you'll have to have your .mobi and .epub files ready to upload here. But, they sell in more formats than anyone else, so if you have fans that still read on their Palm Pilot, they can get books here in all of these formats: Palm DOC/iSolo (PDB), Microsoft Reader (LIT), Franklin eBookman (FUB), Hiebook (KML), Mobipocket (PRC), Rocket (RB), HTML, Adobe (PDF), and Open eBook (epub). They can also automatically email Kindle format books (Mobi) directly to the customer's Kindle.

They pay 60% on all sales and pay quarterly, 45 days after the end of the quarter.

There are tons of other smaller e-book sellers, some of which allow self-pubbers and some that don't. If you know of one, it doesn't hurt to ask if you can put your shingle up there.

I might get in trouble for this, but I'm going to tell you anyway. I recommended staying far away from AuthorSolutions and its subsidiaries, BookTango, Trafford and iUniverse. In my opinion they are the same as the vanity publishers of old. BookTango does offer free DIY and they say their royalties are 100%. I don't see how that works. Just remember when publishing, the money should be flowing to you, not away. If you have to pay to get your book for sale (aside from editing, cover, formatting, etc.) then something is wrong.

I suggest you sign up for an account and self-publish to each retailer individually. Why? More control, more money. However, you can use a distributor for your e-books.

Distributors and Aggregators

This is where your need to evaluate your own personal time-equals-money equation.

Places like Smashwords, Bookbaby, and Draft to Digital (D2D), and XinXii can distribute your book to multiple outlets, like Amazon, Barnes & Noble, Kobo, Apple iBooks and a whole bunch of others I've never heard of. They'll take a cut, but you only have to format and upload your book one time. Remember you'll do a majority of your sales on Amazon, so consider if the ten percent of your sales on those other platforms is worth the time and effort to upload to each of them or if it's better to have someone else distribute to them for you.

You'll have to wait longer to get paid, and you won't make as much because they have wait to get paid and take their cut. Plus, most distributors only pay quarterly, whereas the retailers mostly all pay monthly.

I personally didn't have much luck using a distributor. Their formatting meatgrinder literally made me cry and I sold three whole books in the first month. Probably because it took three weeks for my book, and then even longer for the cover to appear on the retailers' websites.

For me, it's worth it to have that direct control over my books, have more real times sales data and the ability to make changes almost instantly instead of waiting for weeks. But, it also takes me an extra couple of days to upload to each site, enter all the metadata and prices, and make sure everything looks right.

Smashwords

They've always been there for the self-pubbers and if you want, they can distribute your book to all the majors, except Amazon, for a cut. They have great relationships with all kinds of platforms you can't get into, so even if you're uploading directly to Amazon, B&N, iBooks etc., you can still take advantage of the other places they distribute to like Baker and Taylor, OverDrive, and Library Direct.

Smashwords will allow you to price your book to free, which is great when you're trying to get Amazon to price match, and they offer the ability to set your book up for pre-order on some of the retailers.

The hardest part of Smashwords is formatting to their style guide. Your Word file has to be mega clean and if it's not perfect you won't be able to get into their premium catalog. Only premium status books can be distributed out to the other retailers. Mark Coker does provide a style guide for formatting which includes the fabled hug-a-loved-one nuclear method for cleaning up your document. Good luck.

Smashwords offers royalties of 60% of list price from major e-book retailers and 85% net from sales directly from Smashwords with some exceptions. They pay quarterly because they have to wait for their payments from the retailers first.

Draft to Digital (D2D)

Out of all the publishing aggregators, I hear the best things about D2D. They don't have a style guide that makes you cry trying to adhere to it, they have almost real time sales reporting, and most importantly, they pay monthly, assuming you make the minimum payment threshold. They'll let you use the epub file they create from your Word doc anywhere else you'd like. So you can upload it to other retailers they don't distribute to.

Their fees for most retailers channels is approximately 10% of the retail price (it's technically 15% of the net royalties) and they distribute to iBooks, Barnes & Noble, Kobo, Page Foundry, Scribd, and CreateSpace.

XinXii

This a German e-book distributor, sort of like Germany's Smashwords. They aren't very big yet, but Germans read a super mega ton of books, so if you're planning a global marketing strategy (or have your books in foreign translations) you should look at putting your books up for sale here.

They are also a great option for people who don't have a US Tax ID (and don't want one.) XinXii's royalties are 70% of net sales for books priced over EUR 1.99 / US$ 2.49 / £ 1.59. You'll get 40% of net sales for everything priced at or between EUR 0.99 and EUR 1.98 / US$ 0.99 and US$ 2.48 / £ 0.89 and £ 1.58 when you sell through XinXii. They pass on about 85% for sales through their distribution partners.

Make sure you sign up for XinXii Power or XinXii Plus for extended distribution. It's free for fiction books, but there's a charge for non-fiction.

Your own website

You've also got the option of selling your book on your own website. This requires quite a bit of work because you'll need set up an ecommerce page and track and pay all the sales tax. But, you'll also get to keep 100% of the sale, not share the royalties with a seller.

Print sales.

Umm... you got me. Just kidding. Sort of. For most of us small fish in the sea, print books are not nearly as lucrative or as easy to get into reader's hands as e-books.

As a self-published author, you're likely having your books printed on-demand (POD). It's cheaper and easier than trying to get a mass print run from a printer and then storing a bunch of books in your garage.

There are quite few companies out there that would love to help you print your book, but they are not all created equal. Be really wary of vanity publishers who want to charge you upfront to make your book for sale.

When choosing your print-on-demand company, you will need to decide if you want distribution through them too. Some on demand printers don't make your book available to purchase except by you. That's fine if you want one or two copies for yourself, but not if you want to sell the print version of your book

CreateSpace

This is Amazon's Print on Demand (POD) arm. Payments are slightly more complicated, as it's calculated on your royalty minus a fixed charge per book and a per page charge per book. In the CreateSpace store your royalty is 80%, on Amazon it's 60% and through CreateSpace's expanded distribution channels it's 40%.The current fixed charges are from $0.85-$3.65 depending on print color and length, and the per page charge is none to $0.07 per page, again depending on color and book length. CreateSpace has a detailed explanation page and a royalty calculator here - https://www.createspace.com/royalties.

They pay approximately two months after the end of the month.

Create Space is the vendor of choice for a lot of indie authors because they make the process so darn easy and your book goes up for sale on Amazon quickly. The one downside is that it's hard to get your book for sale anywhere else. A lot of vendors won't carry Create Space books because they don't want to support Amazon.

Lightning Source/IngramSpark

These guys are the alternative to CreateSpace. LSI will only work with authors with at least ten or more books to put out all in one go. They aren't set up for the average self-publisher.

You probably want to go with IngramSpark. They have a $49 set up fee unless you order 50 books, and then they'll give you a refund. They have some reach that CreateSpace doesn't because they aren't an Amazon company. (Yes, there are plenty of places that won't sell CreateSpace books because they don't want to support Amazon.)

When your books are sold through their distribution partners you are paid 45% or 60% of the list price minus print costs, depending on your wholesale discount. They pay within 90 days depending on when they get the money.

The downside of distributing your book through Ingram is that it's harder to get through Amazon. It may show out of stock or give a two to three week delay time.

Lulu

The POD publisher that makes it easy to make hardcover books. They have extended distribution if your book meets their guidelines. Their one quirk is that they pay through PayPal and usually 45 days after the end of the month.

It's hard to find their royalties because they want you to use their revenue calculator, but it seems to be about 30%, but don't forget they deduct for the printing and distribution fees.

BookBaby, Books-a-million, and Lulu all offer printing but not distribution (although Lulu offers both options), so look into them if you only want a few copies and not looking to have the print books for sale.

There are other print publishers out there and they all have different deals. Research them carefully to see their printing costs, distribution fees, royalties, and available distribution channels before signing up with anyone.

The last option is only available to prolific, best-selling self-published author like Bella Andre and Barbara Freethy. You can sign a deal with a publisher for print only rights. But, because these authors are blazing the trails someday, it will be an option for us all.

Setting up your accounts

This took me longer to do than I thought it would so I decided it was important to include in the guide.

You'll need some basic information to set up your accounts with all the retailers.

Your Company/Publisher information:

For most people this us just your name, or your pen name. If you've established a publishing company, which can be a sole proprietorship, an LLC, or other kind of corporation, you can put that information here.

The rest of the information is just your address. If Amazon is going to send you anything, this is where you want it sent.

Your Tax information

Who's paying the taxes on the money you earn selling your book on Amazon? It's probably you, personally, unless you've set up a corporation of some sort. You need to list the legal name that is going to appear on your tax returns here.

Why? Amazon is going to send you a 1099 form at the beginning of the year that says how much money they gave you. Yes, you have to pay taxes on that money. (Go get yourself a tax person to help you with that, please, I'm begging you. It's not that expensive, I promise.)

A bank account

I know it's scary to be giving a giant company like Amazon your banking info, but this is how you will be paid. Think of it like a direct deposit from an employer. (But, it's not, it's your royalties - see above about getting a tax person).

You can get paid by a check, but there's a minimum dollar threshold that you must cross in earnings before they'll send your money out that way, and I don't recommend it.

You'll need your account number and your bank's routing number. The easiest place to find this is on the bottom of your checks or deposit slips. If not, pop into the bank, they'll give you the info. You might even be able to get your bank's routing number online. That's where I found mine.

Be sure this info is absolutely correct, because this is where Amazon is going to send your money!

You might want to get an account specifically for your business. Most banks will give you a secondary account. It will make it easier at tax time to track your income and expenditures if you have separate business and personal accounts. Not necessary, but something to think about.

A very few places will pay into a PayPal account, so you might want to set one up now if you don't already use one.

Your social security number or Tax ID number

I know, also scary. But, they need this for that 1099 form. Give it up, or they won't give you the money.

An email address

Sounds silly because if you're like me you already have more than one email address. This should be your professional author email and something that you can easily remember and you'll check.

Where to sign away your life

Here's a quick checklist of all the accounts you'll likely be setting up

Amazon

Amazon Author Central (and all the other country Author Central sites)

Kindle Direct Publishing

B&N

Kobo

Apple iBooks

Google Play

CreateSpace

Smashwords

Bowker

PayPal

Getting your book into bookstores.

This is the hardest part of being an independent self-published author. To understand why it's hard to get your book into bookstores you need to understand a little about how they work.

Bookstores, like Barnes & Noble order their books through a distributor, a distributor works directly with the publishers to get their books and warehouse them.

The buyer for the bookstore looks through a catalog from the publishers (or maybe actually gets to talk to a sales person from the publisher who talks up the books they paid the most for and think will make that money back) and chooses the titles they will stock and how many they want. They'll usually buy less books from a debut author than a well-established selling author, and they will definitely check how the last book sold before placing the order.

Because the bookstores can return unsold books to the publisher, their risk is nil if the title isn't selling well.

We self publishers are mostly using the POD model, so once it printed, somebody has to pay for the book. Thus, a bookstore can't return it. Most aren't willing to take that risk.

To get into bookstores you either have to make a deal with a distributor, or create a personal relationship with the bookstore owners. But, don't worry. Just because your book isn't on the shelf at Barnes and Noble doesn't mean you aren't going to sell any books. Remember this is the digital age and almost everybody reads digitally, even they don't, I bet they know how to buy and order your book online.

Sell your book abroad

Foreign Rights are one of the ways you can get your books sold in other countries. If you sell your foreign rights to your book you will probably need to use an agent. When you sell the rights, you are essentially signing up with a publisher in another country. Book sales are huge in Germany, followed by France, and strangely Brazil in Portuguese. Spanish translated books aren't quite there yet but they will be.

Similarly, but separate are foreign translations. Some authors are having their books translated and then selling them through the same retailers as their English language books. Don't think you can just go to Google translate and get yourself a foreign translation copy. It's a whole lot harder than that. You have to hire a professional translator who understands your genre and literature in general. The process isn't easy and it's expensive, so unless you're bilingual or you're independently wealthy, maybe wait until you've made a chunk of change from publishing and you're ready to re-invest in your business.

A Marketing Plan

Some pre-launch research and marketing will help you to be ready to successfully launch your book on release day.

A competitive analysis can help you determine a lot of information that is crucial to the success of your book. You can download a detailed book competitive analysis on my website, www.coffeebreakpublishing.com.

A competitive analysis

Why do an analysis? You need to be an expert on books like yours. Look at things like price, cover style, word count/page numbers/ book blurbs and titles.

You want your book to be what readers expect of your genre. If you write romance are you going to have a manly chest on your cover or maybe an ocean sea scape with a couple dancing in the surf? If you write health and diet how-to's will you have your own picture on that cover? See, you need to know these things.

Use your own book to help you sell more books.

How? Back matter. It can be a great selling tool.

Back matter is all that stuff after The End. What you put back there matters. Whatever you put, it should help you sell more books, but not in a pushy way.

Your back matter shouldn't take up more than 10% of your total page count. That irritates readers because they think they've got a whole lot more story to read, but when they get to the end they find a bunch of other stuff. Not good. Keep what's back there to a minimum.

Here's my list of recommended back matter.

A Thank You from the Author letter.

Say hi, mention something you liked about these characters or about writing this particular book. Then thank your readers and ask them to review the book. You'll get more reviews by simply asking, than if you don't. Reviews sell books.

A sign up for your new releases newsletter.

Building an email list should be a high priority, because if people sign up for your email list because they read the book and found the link in the back, they really do want to know more about you and your next release. A great way to build your list is by offering bonus materials - a short story, an interview with your characters, maybe a follow up post script about what's going on with characters from another story in the same series once they sign up for the newsletter.

A list of your other books with links.

Yes, you'll have to update each of your books with the updated list and buy links each time you release a new book, but again, if they read this book, liked it, and want to read more from you, here's the best opportunity to give them a link to buy the next book (or the first book) right now. If you can keep them short, you could include a few of the book blurbs in your list.

Use your affiliate links so you get paid and/or bit.ly so you can track how many people click and from where. This is traditionally at the front of the book in traditional print, but most e-book readers skip the front matter of a book and start right at the beginning of your first chapter, so it works better as back matter in an e-book.

A preview or excerpt of another book.

The first chapter of the next book in the series. If it hasn't come out yet this can help generate buzz for it now, and if it is available now or for pre-order, that preview should come with a link at the end to buy it or the first book if your series is very long.

If you've got a longer series going, it's a great idea to include a preview for the first book in the series and ask your readers to check out where it all began. Don't include an excerpt from every book you have out. That's why you have a list of books.

This could also be the place to include a preview for a book of an author you are cross promoting with. You include their preview and say something about how you liked it and think your readers would too, and that author does the same for you. That's powerful marketing.

Your author bio.

People want to know about you. You're a celebrity now. Include a picture if you feel comfortable doing that and some interesting information about yourself. I hope you already have a great author bio on your website, but if you don't, you'll need to write one now. (And then have someone proof read it for you. Nothing is more embarrassing than having typos in your author bio.)

Do tell us why you like to write what you write, your inspirations, fun facts about you and where you can be found on the web, like your website, Facebook page, the sign up for your author new releases email list (aka - your newsletter) if you have one, etc. Links work great in an e-book, so make sure you add hyperlinks. Give the URLs in your print copy.

Don't tell me you live in North Whoville with your husband, three kids and two dogs. I know you've seen that on other author bios, but did you find that part interesting? No? Me either.

Pre-launch marketing plan

After you figure out the basics of how to position your book well and utilize your front and back matter to help you sell your other books and yourself, you'll still want a pre-launch marketing plan to let people know you've got a book coming out.

Promo (promotion) is all the free things you can do to promote your book. Marketing cost money.

Here are a few promo and marketing ideas to get you started.

Promo

Remember that platform building we talked about. Now is when you benefit from all that work.

Make sure you let those people on your social media networks know your book is coming and then when it's available, but for goodness sakes, don't be a spammy car salesman about it.

Here are a few things to do on social media:

Put small excerpts and quotes from your book, create graphics with those quotes and pictures that represent some aspect of your work. (Try PicMonkey for that.)

Update your cover photo on your fan page and profile page with a picture that spotlights your new release. (Try PicMonkey for that too.).

Add an excerpt or first chapter of the book for people to read. I like the Freebooksy app for that.

Create a #hashtag for your book using the title, a character's name, your name, or some exciting bit of the plot (but, keep it short). Then post or tweet lines from the book using the hashtag, and don't forget the release date.

Don't forget about your website.

Whether you use blogging to promote your books or not, I hope you have a blog on your site to keep your fans updated on new releases.

Do a cover reveal.

Post your first chapter (you might also do this on the books page of your website.)

Post excerpts to get people enticed with your great writing and story. You can excerpt up to 20% of your book before the retailers make a fuss.

None of those take any extra writing from you, so they are easy posts.

Blog tours are the new book tours. No travel, except online. A blog tour is where you visit the blogs and give them an interview, excerpt, anecdote, deleted scenes, guest post, or anything else that their readers might enjoy. I recommend scheduling the blog tour for the two weeks after your book releases. But to do that, you'll need to talk to bloggers and reviewers a minimum of three months prior to your release. You can do this yourself by contacting your writer friends, the owners of blogs you know and read or submitting to book review sites. Many reviewers want an ARC (Advanced Readers Copy) of the book several months before the release date so they have time to read it and write a review. Everybody likes a book giveaway, so offer that and maybe some swag, like bookmarks or the like for the blogger to giveaway (although you should take responsibility for shipping or emailing the prizes.)

If you don't have the time, there are a lot of blog tour companies out there that can help you for a fee. I've seen as cheap as $20 all the way up to the thousands.

Be sure you schedule the time to participate in the blog tour. You'll have to get your excerpts, bio, headshot, book cover and blog posts ready around two weeks in advance. During the tour you'll need to stop by the different blogs and respond to questions and comments.

I consider book giveaways somewhere in between promo and marketing. Yes, it costs you money, the cost of the book if you're doing print copies, or gifting the e-book through a retailer, the cost of any other items you're giving away, like gift certificates or other prizes, and the cost of mailing. But, book giveaways are a great way to get reviews and start that elusive word of mouth buzz. Before you spend any marketing dollars consider how many books you could give away to readers for the same price?

Goodreads, Shelfari and BookThing all have book giveaways too, although Goodreads only allows print copies. You can schedule a giveaway as soon as you have an ISBN or ASIN number. I recommend doing the giveaway for at least a month, but not longer than three, and at least a month before your release date. If you can do the giveaway prior to release, even by one day. You don't want anyone who might buy it to wait around to see if they've won it.

If you blog or have a news/announcements page on your website be sure to do a post for your pre-release to give everyone the date your book is coming out, and another on release day. Give away a few copies of the print or e-book on your website. I recommend using something like Rafflecopter to make it easy. Be sure to post about your giveaway on your social media outlets too.

Marketing:

Here are some low ticket quick and easy marketing options you can try for pre-launch.

Boosting a post on Facebook. The post when you upload your book cover or link to your book's page on the Amazon will only reach a few people. Stupid Facebook. So, pay to boost it. Five to ten bucks will really expand your reach.

You can also run an ad on Facebook. Don't spend too much money because the effectiveness of this isn't very well proven. The best ad to run pre-launch isn't for the book, but for your author fan page or website. You're trying to build a base of people you can reach using social media when the book comes out.

In the Publish your Book section and in the Post-publication section there are more ideas for specific ideas to do on release day and for continued promotion and marketing. Try creating a marketing checklist of all the things you need and want to do to prepare and promote your book. Then check them off as you go.

Writing your book blurb

Besides the cover, your book blurb is one of the strongest tools you have for getting people to buy your book. Writing copy is not an easy task, and half-assing it when you're tired of fighting with the book sellers trying to get your book uploaded is no time to try and write it up. Have your blurb ready before you even begin so you can easily copy and paste it in.

I recommend you write a short synopsis of your book before you write your blurb, especially if you've written a 100,000 word book. It's going to be hard to whittle that down to 250 words or less.

I like Michael Hague's book Selling Your Story in 60 Seconds and his blog post Elements of the Pitch for a great template for a short synopsis.

Besides helping you write your book blurb, the synopsis will come in handy when you're talking to people about your book. Anytime someone ask you what your book is about you'll be prepared. Don't get caught saying, "Uh...it's about a guy, who does some stuff."

Write this longer synopsis first and then use it to pare down the description to the most basic elements of it to come up with your 250 word blurb.

Yep, you read that right. Your book blurb should be really short. Use this simple formula.

1. A hooking headline
2. Book quotes, reviews or testimonials from other authors or readers
3. The book description
4. The call to action

When you're writing these elements you want to consider the four "U's" of copywriting. Make it:

Urgent

Unique

Ultra-Specific

Useful

The Hooking Headline

Just like that first line and first chapter of your book needs to hook the reader into the story, your headline should hook the reader into either reading more about it or buying it. A huge majority of people won't read more than the headline, so it's the part of the blurb you want to spend the most time creating.

Think about what need your book fulfills for the reader. You may want to write your headline as a question. Make sure the answer to that question is yes. It's a psychological thing. You want them to say yes to your question and yes to your book.

Your headline and call to action should address these questions.

How is your book USEFUL to the reader?

How is your book UNIQUE?

Answer those questions in and ULTRA-SPECIFIC way, and try to create a sense of URGENCY.

The story summary

This is not a book report. You're only allowed (by me) to write two short paragraphs as most here. Yeah, I know there's no way to get your whole story in that short amount of space. That's not the point. You're only want to entice them into reading to see what happens.

The call to action

Yes, actually tell people to buy your book. Right now, today,

Make your book description stand out.

People are very visual creatures, so make sure your book blurb looks appealing. On Amazon and NookPress you can use some HTML to make your description look fabulous. Amazon has its own special html language, so here's a few tricks for writing your book description and making it great.

Use a different style for your hooking headline. Make it bold, italicized, a bigger font, or a larger size font than the rest of the blurb.

Here's some really basic information on using HTML to format your description.

You have to use an opening tag, for example <b> and a closing tag, for example </b>). You would put your text between the two tags alter it.

To make your text Bold you would write it like this: <b> your text </b>. Everything that is in between these tags will appear in bold text.

This is the tag for a line break: Line Break: <br>. You can insert these to add some white space in your description, like when you have more than one paragraph.

Bullet Point Lists: <ul>, <ol> & <li>

These are the tags needed to create bullet or numbered points.

The UL tag stands for unordered list and everything in between them will be put in bullet points. The LI tags are there to differentiate the different bullet points. It's easier to understand when you see it.

The bullet point list:

<ul>

<li> Bullet point #1 </li>

<li> Bullet point # 2 </li>

</ul>

On your Amazon page it will look like this:

Bullet point #1

Bullet point #2

The OL tag instead of UL tag makes numbered bullet points.

The numbered bullet point list:

<ol>

<li> Bullet point #1 </li>

<li> Bullet point # 2 </li>

</ol>

And this would create:

Bullet point # 1

Bullet point # 2

There is a whole slew of HTML tags that you can use, and the list can be found in the KDP help topics at https://kdp.amazon.com/help?topicId=A377RPHW6ZG4D8.

A few other common ones are:

<em> italic text

<h2>, <h3>, <h4>, <h5> for headings. H2 is the heading for the Amazon Orange heading.

Pricing

How do you decide how much to charge for your book?

Start with a competitive analysis. Look at the prices of other books that are like yours. Factors when choosing antecedents are format, genre, length, how many books the author has available, what book this it is in a series and how long it's been available. Also, check to see if it's on sale.

There's a full competitive analysis you can download for free on my website at www.CoffeeBreakPublishing.com.

Check your competitive analysis to make sure you are priced strategically. If most books in your category sell for $7.99 and your book's price is $2.99 or $15.99 something is wrong.

Generally, fiction books cost less than non-fiction, e-books cost less than print. Beyond that, you'll want to pay attention to trends. For example, right now there is a trend to sell box sets of around six to ten books for $0.99 cents. Ain't nobody making any money off that. (They're doing it as a marketing and promotion tool.) Readers have come to expect that a box set like that will be inexpensive.

The sweet spots I'm seeing right now for full length (50-100K words) genre fiction is an e-book from $2.99-$5.99. A lot of genre fiction authors are offering novellas (under 40K words) for anywhere from $0.99 to $2.99. I've also seen a slew of short stories (under 10K words) being offered for the same prices points.

You have to decide how much your work is worth. On the one hand you don't want to under value your work, but on the other hand you have to price competitively.

You also want to take royalties into consideration. Most of the retailers pay a flat royalty rate, but Amazon, which is where you'll sell most of your books, has two.

The 35% royalty is for books priced below $2.99 or above $9.99 USD. It is also for books sold in the Indian, Japanese, Mexican and Brazilian stores no matter the price if your book is not enrolled in KDP select.

You can earn 70% royalties on your book if it is priced from $2.99 to $9.99. Right now that's the most out of all the major self-publishing platforms. Cool.

The small caveat to the 70% royalty option is that Amazon charges you, the author, a small delivery fee. The fee depends on the size of your book file. In the US store it will cost you $0.15 per megabyte of the .mobi file, with a minimum of $0.01. (So compress those pictures to reduce your files size!)

If your book is very picture heavy and a very large file it might be more cost efficient for you to choose the 35% royalty structure. You can still price your book between $2.99 and $9.99, but won't be charged any delivery fee.

Why the major difference. Amazon thinks that books priced in that 70% royalty range sell the best and make the most money. Do $0.99 books sell a lot? Sure they do, but they are a lot of work for everyone for that ninety-nine cents, so not as worth it to Amazon.

Let's look at the price difference in a $0.99 book vs a $2.99 cent book.

One book at $0.99 earns you $0.3465.

One book at $2.99 earns you $2.093 minus your delivery charge.

You'd need to sell about six books at $0.99 to make the same money as one $2.99 book.

I recommended calculating your break even. Say your book cost you $500 to produce, a hundred for your cover and three-hundred for your editing, the rest, like your formatting and such, a hundred - good job. If you charge $0.99 for your book you need to sell a little over 1400 books to break even, but at $2.99 you only need to sell 240. How many books do you think you can sell and how long will it take you do it? That's where you breakeven price point is.

Formatting

The formats you'll want are:

.mobi for sale on Amazon

.epub for sale almost everywhere else, NookPress (Barnes & Noble), iBooks, Kobo

.pdf, most a lot e-readers like the Kindle and the Nook can also read PDF files. This is also the format you'll need for your print book.

A few other formats that are still available for e-readers, but getting closer to obsolescence, so you can make them (or have them made) if you want, but don't feel obligated to do more than the basic three above.

The easiest place to write your manuscript is probably Microsoft Word. It's also very easy to upload a word .doc or .docx file to KDP and have them turn it into a .mobi file, which is what Kindle books are, or to NookPress and have them turned it into an epub, which makes up most e-books.

What you see on the Word page will be really similar to what you see in the e-book.

If you and Microsoft Word are mortal enemies you can also upload an HTML file to KDP. Some authors swear this is the only way to get a really clean e-book. The downside is you have to know HTML. It's this whole other language. I know the basics, but ee-gads, I couldn't even possibly begin to look at an entire book in an HTML file format. If you're comfortable with HTML, feel free to export your Word doc into an HTML file and have at it. If you've got a very complex book with charts and pictures you might need to go the HTML route, but you can still start with a Word doc.

Follows some simple guidelines and you won't have to worry (as much) about the formatting.

Use styles not manual formatting.

You know when you want to indent your first line and you press the space key five-ish times?

STOP THAT RIGHT NOW.

You're using manual formatting. Same goes for hitting the Enter/Return key a bunch of times to get to the next page. *shiver*

Word has some formatting you need to learn to use. Start by turning on the Show/Hide formatting feature in your Word document. It's that button that looks like a giant backwards P.

Now you can see all of your paragraph breaks, spaces and other formatting.

If you're using an even vaguely recent version of Word you should see the Styles box on your home tab. Word has set you up with some basic formatting styles. Look under the Design tab for some different themes. Feel free to play with them, but some use fancy fonts and you don't want that in your e-book, I promise.

I can't go into all the details of styles here because that would be its very own book. Google or YouTube how-to use styles in MS Word and you'll find tons of help. If you are a Word guru, you can easily create your own styles in Word and more power to ya. Just remember to keep it simple.

Using styles will also make creating your Table of Contents easy-peasy.

You can create and insert a TOC (Table of Contents) from the Reference tab in Word. Amazon wants you to have one, so do it the easy way! (Except for Smashwords - don't get me started). Just click on the table of contents button and pick one of the styles. Then be sure to update the field if you're missing any chapters or the page numbers aren't correct.

Always use a very common font like Times New Roman or Arial. I know they aren't the prettiest, but most e-book devices can't ready anything but the most basic of fonts anyway. If you use a fancy font it will be converted to something simple and if there are characters that can't be read in that conversion they are going to look like weird boxes and funny symbols. You don't want that.

The print version of your book can use fancier styles and fonts. You'll be uploading a PDF document to most of the on demand self-publishing platforms like CreateSpace or Lulu, which is kind of like a digital picture. They print what they see. Kind of (it's way more complex than that, but if you really want to know, Google it, you'll find all kinds of info to crowd your brain.)

Don't use tables. They don't show up right on e-readers. If you absolutely need a table in your book, you'll want to include it as a picture. Try converting your table to an image first.

Pictures should be .jpeg format for the best results. You'll want to insert the photo instead of copy and pasting it. (Nobody really knows why, just go with it, so you don't have any problems). Your pictures also need to be formatted to be in-line with the text. I know it looks prettier to have the pictures all over the place and the text next to it, but the e-readers can't do it. Save the pretty for your print book.

Your print book is going to need mirror margins with a gutter. This means on the left page the print is slightly to the left and on the right, slightly to the right. That way your words don't get squished into the binding in the middle of the book. The specs for your margins are on the publisher's (CreateSpace, etc.) websites.

Book size

For print, you'll need to decide what size you want your book to be before you can set up the margins. Size matters, not only for your formatting, but for look, feel and marketing too.

The most common size for fiction books you pick up at the store is the Mass Market Paperback. They are 4.25 x 7 inches. Self-publishers generally can't get books cut to this trim. The next most common size is the Trade Paperback. These are the books that are a bit taller than your standard mass market paperback. There's no standard size for these, but they are generally about 5 x 8 to 6 x 9. There are all kinds of choices within that range for you to choose. You'll want to pick depending on the length, word or page count, of your book, the paper choice and your font size. For a 100,000 word novel on cream paper you might want to go slightly bigger and use the 6 x 9, so it doesn't look like I'm carrying around an encyclopedia in my purse.

If you've got the paperback version of this book, it's about 25,000 words, black & white interior on cream paper with a trim size of 5.5 x 8.5.

Templates are your friends

If you want to make your life easier, get a template. There are a few places out there that sell Word doc templates for e-books. The styles, including a table of contents are all set up for you, all you have to do is type. Awesome.

CreateSpace has templates you can download for free. I got my template from Joel Friedlander over at

www.bookdesigntemplates.com. Worth every penny.

File Conversion

Once you're book is written and you've done as much as you can to have a clean Word doc or HTML file it's time to convert it to a format people can buy.

Almost all of the e-book readers can read a PDF file, so if you're selling it yourself or sending out eARCs of your book this is a great option.

To turn your Word document into a PDF file, the easiest way is to do a save as and choose the PDF file type. There are converters available for free online too, but I hope you don't have to do it that way. If you do, try going to the local library and using their computers. They should have a reasonably up to date version of Word that can do a save as to PDF. But, Word isn't Adobe Acrobat Pro. It uses a small chunk of Adobe's program to convert your document into an archival PDF. The problems with an archival PDF is that it doesn't have embedded fonts. That's fine for your e-book, but not for your print. If you use this easy peasy method to get a PDF make sure you look under the options and choose to embed the fonts.

If you want to skip the price of getting your book professionally formatted, you can let the booksellers make e-reader ready your files.

Amazon KDP will make your mobi file from your Word document or HTML file. In fact, they prefer it.

NookPress will make your epub file from your Word doc and let you edit it.

Kobo will make your epub file from your Word doc.

Smashwords will make all the formats from your very clean word doc, but make sure you read Mark Coker's Guide or you'll be in tears in no time. I was.

Here's the thing, epub conversion and files are actually pretty complex and what you put in is going affect what you get. Word has all kinds of weird (but amazing) background stuff going on that no matter how much you clean it up, there will still be some garbage in there that could make your epub file wonky. Make sure you check the files before you approve them. All the platforms have some sort of previewer, or you can download the actual file. They all also have free e-reader programs you can load to your computer, tablet or phone to check them. Check them. It will save you the grief of getting bad reviews because of horrible formatting.

If you're uploading your Word doc to any of the retailers and your file comes out weird, try saving the Word document as an HTML file. If you understand HTML at all, surf through the areas that didn't come out right and see what the code looks like. If you don't understand HTML go on to the next step, which is getting someone else to format your book.

If that scares you enough and you've got a little extra money, you can pay someone to format your book and present you with a beautiful e-book or PDF file for print.

Fiverr is a cool website where you can hire people to do all kinds of things for you at the cost of $5. They almost all offer additional services for more money, so check their gig details closely. There are a lot of Fiverr's offering services to writers and formatting is just one of them. Just remember, you get what you pay for.

Marie Force, who is a self-publishing Goddess, has developed some services for other writers that she's needed over the years. Check out her Formatting Fairies at:

BB e-books is this cool guy who lives in Thailand and can format your e-books beautifully. Find him at www.bbebooksthailand.com.

If you want to do the formatting yourself, there are some software programs out there to purchase. Some are really expensive with a big learning curve and others are cheap and easy. Remember, once again, you get what you pay for and I can't guarantee any of them will make the perfect epub file, but I know authors and small publishers who use any and all of these with successful results.

Check out:

InDesign - a fancy publishing program from Adobe. You can get a free one month trial to see if you can work with it, and then pay per month to use it.

Jutoh - a great little basic e-book creation program. I know a lot of self-publishers that use it to format their books and have no problems at all. It has a free trail and isn't very expensive.

Scrivener - Yep, that same program that you can write in can also create your e-books. Best to check out some online tutorials to figure out how though

Calibre - This free program was really designed to store and catalog all your e-books, but it's got some extra features for formatting that you might find useful.

Sigil - No matter the program you use to convert your manuscript to an e-book you'll probably still need to edit the file. None of the programs that convert will make a totally clean book. Sigil is an epub editor that you can use to do that. Unfortunately it's no longer supported, but all the epub editor gurus out there still love and use it.

There are places you can convert your Word doc or HTML file to an epub on the web, but if you don't also have an epub editing program they won't be much good, because they don't produce very good looking books.

No matter the way you get your epub files you need to check them for problems. EPUB Validator is an online tool from IDPF that will "validate" your EPUB. It makes sure that the file has all the right epub specifications. The check errors are hard to interpret and the best way to figure out what they mean is to Google them. If something is wrong when you get your results back, you'll probably have issues when you go to upload to the retailers.

Updating your files.

One of the perks of e-publishing and even on demand is that you can update your book as often as you want. When your next book comes out you can automatically update the lists of your works and the links to them in your front and back matter.

If you're doing some cross promoting with another author, you can add a book blurb or an excerpt in your back matter for a short time. It's a cool way to keep up to date in today's fast paced world. Beware that if you change more than ten percent of the book, you'll need a new ISBN. Check the section on ISBNs for more information.

What to include in the book besides the story

Front Matter is all the stuff at the front of the book before chapter one. Open up any print book and you'll see a whole plethora of front matter. Here are the basics of what you need in your book.

A Title page with your book's title and your author name

Pick a nice, big, bold font size for your title under, than choose a slightly smaller font for your name. Do not include the word "by" before your name, that's only for unpublished manuscripts.

You might also include your publishing company name if you've formed one (see the business plan section) and the city of your publishing company.

A copyright page including and All Rights Reserved statement and a publisher's note

Along with the copyright symbol you can include the word "copyright" then your name (or pen name - see the ISBN section for more information about copyrighting with a pen name). I also suggest and "All Rights Reserved" paragraph.

It's not strictly necessary, but it reiterates that you know and understand your IP rights. Be sure to list your name (or pen name), your publishing company and some contact information should someone actually ask permission to use a portion of your book for something beyond a review. You may list an address they can physically write to (but, I'd only do that if you have a P.O. Box set up for your business). I just included my website because there is a contact form there and if someone really wants to get a hold of me they can do it there.

Publisher's note.

This is that bit that says you made everything up and didn't base it on anybody real. It's a modicum of protection against getting sued for libel, slander, or defamation. Of course, it doesn't do you a bit of good if you really did commit any of those.

Other Copyrights

Next you should list any other copyrights that are relevant to the book. If you had someone design the interior, had someone design the cover, used any photographs or images that you didn't create, those should all be listed as copyrights.

The one that I've been seeing that isn't copyrightable is editing. That editor didn't create your words, they might have helped you make them better, but that doesn't count. Don't give them a copyright. You can thank them in your acknowledgments though.

End your copyright page with the edition information which includes the book title, your name and the edition number. The ISBN, if you have one accompanies the edition number (because different editions of a book get different ISBNs). If you chose not to get an ISBN for your e-book you can list the ASIN or other retailer identifier there instead.

An example copyright page:

Acknowledgments page

This is that short (keep it to one page) thank you letter at the beginning of a book that gives a shout out to all the people that helped you make it happen. Yay team!

A Dedication page

You don't need a dedication page, but it's my favorite part. Dedicate your book to your mom, your husband, your dog, all the people in the world like you, or even yourself.

You might even say why you're dedicating to someone if you want to make me cry a little bit. I love dedication pages. Yeah, I'm weird like that.

Other Titles

Next up is a list of other titles by you. If it's in the e-book make sure to put in the hyperlink to where ever they can be bought, like the Amazon, Barnes & Noble, iBooks page, etc.

Only insert links for the place you're uploading that particular book. Barnes & Noble gets pretty pissed if you put Amazon links in a book they have for sale and vice versa. This is the place to use your affiliate program links so you get some extra mula on the sale of the book. Yeah, baby.

If you have other books out this is also the place to put praise for those books, but don't go crazy or people won't look at them.

In the print version this typically goes in the front of the book, but in your e-book, you can put it in the front or the back.

The Table of Contents

This can make or break your book when you're trying to upload it. You need a linkable table of contents, meaning if I see the words Chapter One, you better be able to click on them and be taken directly to chapter one.

Word can create one for you. Check the formatting section for more information.

Back Matter is all the stuff that comes after 'The End'. Don't forget about these things because back matter sells books (especially once you have more than one book out).

A Thank You Letter

Try out a thank you from the author letter. Thank the reader for taking this little journey with you and if they enjoyed it, ask them to leave your a review. That might sound strange, but we all know that reviews sell books, and you'll get more reviews if you specifically ask for them. You can even put a clickable link to the review page you want them to use right here to make it even easier.

Let the reader's know what's coming up next from you or in the series (with a clickable link in the e-book. The link can lead directly to the book's sale page, or if it's out, to the pre-order page, or your website.) You might also include here where they can go to sign up for your new releases newsletter and other places to contact you like your website and your social media.

Excerpts and Previews

You might also include an excerpt or the first chapter of one of your other books. If you've got a series, the next book in the series, or if it's a long running series, maybe the first book with a note about seeing where it all began.

This is a great way to do some cross-promotion with other authors. You put their book blurbs and links in the back of your e-book and they do the same for you. Then hopefully you both gain some new readers.

List of other Titles

Put a list of all books, with links in the e-book directly to the book's sale page for the site this book is available on (If they bought it at B&N make sure the link it for the B&N sales page, etc.).

You may also want to put some sort book blurbs along with the list or some sort excerpts. But don't go crazy here. If you're going to do blurbs and/or excerpts stick with no more than three. You don't want your back matter to take up more than about 10% of the book because that just irritates readers.

Book Cover

Don't fool yourself into believing that people don't judge a book by its cover. They totally do. Your cover will sell more books than any marketing and promo you do and probably even more than your content. Don't get me wrong, if your content is crappy you probably won't continue to sell books and if it is you will. But, if you have a lame homemade cover and great content you're going to have a hard time reaching as many people as you want.

So, my advice is to hire a professional cover artist. Someone who actually knows about designing book covers, not your cousin who is taking a graphic design class.

A professional cover can cost anywhere from $16 to $5000. But, a good average price is around $125-$150.

Pre-made covers are a great way to go. They're usually about half the price of a custom covers and a lot of times they are fantastic because these are often the projects graphic designers work on when they are practicing new techniques or styles.

The downside is you have limited input into the design and changes.

Don't accept a bad cover, if you and the designer didn't have the same vision, let them know. Be nice. Don't tell them their cover is cheesy or corny. You also want to make sure that your cover looks good in multiple sizes. At most retailers and on reading devices your readers and potential customers are only going to see the small icon. Be sure you can still read the title and/or your name on that small picture too.

Think about trying to brand yourself through your covers. You want some cover continuity, same font for your name, same look for where you name and the title goes, etc. This is especially important when you've got a series. You want people to know which books are in the series just by the continuity of covers.

No matter where you get your cover be sure you attribute the right people. If someone designs your cover, list that person on the copyright page. If they used photos or images that the two of you didn't create, or get royalty free, list the photographer or artist on your copyright page too.

Do your research.

First you should look at other popular titles in your genre. Make note of the ones you like and why. Also check out designs you hate and why.

Next research artists. There is a whole Internet full of people who are selling book covers. Choose wisely. Any artist worth their fees will have a portfolio of designs they have done for other authors. If you find some you really like contact the authors via social media and ask about their experience with the artist. The writing community is pretty open and helpful, so most people will be happy to talk to you.

Print vs E-book

You'll need a very different cover file for your e-book vs your print book. The print cover will be an extra charge and will cost you more than the e-book file, because frankly, it's a lot more work for the designer to do. It needs to be higher resolution and fit into horribly specific templates, otherwise your spine is halfway into your back cover and your picture comes out blurry. You don't want that, so fork over the extra money.

A note on cover art. If your cover is too sexy you'll have a harder time selling it because the retailers won't merchandise your book (which is where they do a little extra promotion to tell they're readers about a book like putting it into a Summer Reads or an new releases email blast or something. You can't buy merchandising, it's part of their own internal marketing programs.) They'll flag your book as adult content, they'll bury you, they'll stick you in the never to see the light of day or be found until page twenty-three of a search. So, be careful and keep that in mind. I'm not saying don't put the sexy man chest on your sexy novel but be aware of how you'll be strategically placing your book underneath the bed up in the attic.

ISBNs

To ISBN or Not? That is today's question.

What's an ISBN?

ISBN stands for International Standard Book Number. It's thirteen digits long and uniquely identifies each book. Bookstores and libraries use them to order books and keep track of what they have. There is embedded information in those numbers about where and who published the book.

Where do you get one?

Each country has its own ISBN agency.

In the US you can buy an ISBN from Bowker. They hold a monopoly on ISBNs in the US, so even if you get one through a publisher or self-publishing platform, they got it from Bowker. There are plenty of services that acquire an ISBN, but if you pay more than $125 for one, you got taken.

In Canada, you can get your ISBN from the government http://www.collectionscanada.gc.ca and they're free. Ta da! (I'm moving to Canada.)

In the UK, Nielsen is where you'll get your ISBN from. Read their information here first, because you have to fill out and application and it's all very complicated. http://www.isbn.nielsenbook.co.uk.

In Australia you get Thorpe-Bowker at https://www.myidentifiers.com.au/

In New Zealand the National Library get ISBNs for you. Fill out the form at http://natlib.govt.nz/forms/isn

Do you need one?

For your e-book...no. Each of the self-publishing platforms will assign your book a designator that they will use to track sales in their store. For example, Amazon uses the ASIN number.

You can absolutely just use this designator.

Why wouldn't you want to?

Smashwords requires an ISBN to be added to their premium distribution catalog. If you provide your own, you won't be able to take advantage of their library distribution channels. They are happy to give you a free one, and be listed as your publisher.

Apple no longer requires an ISBN, but they still recommend it. Their publisher guidelines state that they use ISBNs for reporting sales to the major trade publications. If you upload your book without an ISBN, you can't add it later. You would have to upload the ISBN-assigned version of your book as a new product.

Kobo doesn't require an ISBN, but if you provide one you'll be able to take advantage of their big ole network of distributing partners around the world.

If you do buy ISBNs from Bowker be sure to fill out the information on your My Identifiers page as completely as you can. Those records feed to Bowker's Books In Print database, which is huge and used by retailers and libraries all over the place.

What about print books?

If you plan to sell your book through any sort of bookstore, online or brick and mortar, or if you'd like your book to be in libraries. You'll need an ISBN.

Most of the publishing platforms will sell you and ISBN for a greatly reduced price - like around free to $25. There are pros and cons to using their ISBNs.

If you want to be listed as the publisher of your book, you'll want to get your own. ISBNs are sold to publishers (even if that publisher is just the author of the book), and only the publisher who owns the ISBN can be listed as the publisher of the book. So if you published with say, CreateSpace (the print arm of Amazon's self-publishing platform) and use their ISBN they'll provide for free, Amazon is listed as the publisher of your book.

Each format or version of the book needs its own ISBN. So if you have a hardcover, a paperback and an e-book you might have three ISBNs. The great debate right now is whether the different formats of e-books, like Mobi, epub, pdf, etc., need their own ISBNs. Most self-pubbers are saying no, while Bowker says yes, pretty please. You'll need to decide for yourself. Personally, I say an e-book is an e-book, so I only used one. Although Smashwords will ask you to provide a totally separate and unused ISBN for the version you upload to them.

Since I recommend distributing to each of the retailers (Amazon, B&N, etc.) individually if you can, you might as well use Smashwords free ISBN for their site and their extended distribution. More on this in the section on where to sell your books.

One and only

An ISBN can only be used one time, ever. They can never be re-assigned. So, be careful with them.

If you make certain changes to your book, it will need a new ISBN. You need a new ISBN if:

You make significant changes to any part or parts of the book, like as adding new text, moving, or removing blocks of text and/or chapters. The rule of thumb here is if you are changing ten percent, or more of the text you'll need a new ISBN.

You change the title or subtitle

You publish your book in a new product format (hardcover, paperback, e-book, audio book, etc.).

You create and publish your work in a new trim size (change the book's dimensions).

You publish with another publisher or under a new imprint.

You issue a translated version of your published work.

You don't need a new ISBN if:

You change the price

You make minor corrections (spelling, grammar, typos) to an existing edition.

CHAPTER FOUR

Publish your book

Push Publish

Phew, you've done everything you need to get ready to release your book. So let's publish.

Just kidding. First I want you to set a release date.

Why not publish that sucker the second it's finished? Release day build-up buzz. You want people to know you've written a book. I hope you've been talking about it on social media all this time. This is even more important for subsequent books. If you do some promo, maybe some marketing, talk about the book on your blog and social media, send out ARCs (Advanced Review Copies) to reviewers you'll get people excited to buy your book. When it goes on sale more people will buy it and your sales ranks will shoot up the charts. The higher your rank, the more people who will see your book and the more people who will buy it. Yay!

If you want to do a book blog with reviews you need to have the book ready at least two months before the release.

Another delay in publishing you might want to consider is to wait and publish a whole slew of books at one time. By doing that you'll be creating an instant backlist. When readers come to buy one of your books, they'll love it, I'm sure, and then they come back to buy more. If you don't have more, well, how sad, for both of you.

Do you have a bunch of manuscripts under the bed from years of writing and being rejected by the publishing establishment? Get them all out, polish them up, and publish them all!

I was lucky enough to attend a workshop by prolific self-published author, Liliana Hart. She recommends having five books out all at once and then one in the hole ready to publish the following month. She credits following that formula as her key to success as a self-published author.

This will work great if you've got a bunch of stuff written already. If you don't, you shouldn't wait too long to publish that first book. Start making some money now, and then try to get the rest of your books out as fast as you can and still have a great product.

You've got your release date set, you're telling people about it, the book is ready to go because you've had it critiqued, professionally edited, you paid for a fantastic cover and the formatting is spot-on. Login to the account you created for the platform you want to sell on and follow the directions. Really.

Most of the publishing websites make it as easy as they can to get your book uploaded and for sale. There's almost always forums or some sort of message boards if you have problems with the process. Some of the publishers have help desks that can walk you through the process too. If you've done all the prep in the writing and pre-publication sections you'll be fine.

If you've planned ahead and have a release date more than two weeks out, you can also set your book for pre-order on a few platforms like Amazon, Kobo, and Smashwords. Don't choose pre-order if your manuscript isn't totally complete. You'll have to upload the final manuscript at least ten days prior to your release date and if you miss the upload date or move your release date you'll get put in pre-order jail, meaning you won't be able to use the perk again.

When you've got everything ready and pretty push publish. Now do the snoopy dance.

On most of the platforms you'll wait about twelve to forty-eight hours before you book becomes live, meaning people can buy it and read it. As soon as your book goes live be sure to go grab those links so you can share them with everyone you know. Congratulations. You're now a published author. Rock on!

Extra information about Amazon

Since you're probably going to publish on Amazon, I thought it was worth it to give you some extra information about them. For even more, check out the Quick Break Guide to Self Publishing on Amazon.

You may love them, you may hate them, but they are the biggest booksellers in the whole wide world, so if you actually want to sell more than a few books, you have to sell them through Amazon. A majority of your book sales will be generated here. If you're rolling your eyes and hating the man, well, effect some change from the inside-out. Sign up, sell your books here and complain all you want to the nice people at the Amazon help desk.

Amazon offers self-published authors the tools to create and sell all three formats, e-book, print and audio.

For your digital books you'll use Kindle Direct Publishing (KDP). You can find them at www.kdp.amazon.com.

KDP offers a program to authors called KDP Select. If you agree to publish on Amazon exclusively for 90 days they will offer you some extra promotional and discovery tools. You can choose the Kindle Countdown Deal where you can put your book on sale and your book's page will have a countdown clock telling customers when the sale ends. You can even do it in graduated steps, for example, $0.99 for a couple days, $1.99 for a few more, $2.99 for a while and then back up to full price. Even at $0.99 you'll make 70% royalties where non Kindle Countdown books priced at $0.99 only make 35%.

Choose between the countdown or free days. Normally Amazon doesn't allow you to price your book at free. They will price match to free if your book is listed on other sites free, but you can't price your book at $0.00. If you choose the free days option on KDP Select, they will give you five free days. Use them all in one chunk or, even better, break them up into one three-day and one two-day chunk so you can run two promotions.

Use your free wisely though. Don't give your book away for nothing. Use free strategically. If you only have one book available, how is it helping you to make money if you put it for free? You might see your book rise up the free book rankings, and some authors see a slight increase in sales after the free promo because of the increase in visibility, but that's going to drop off fast. You might also get a few more reviews because so many people download your free book. Those are both good, but aren't they even better if you see those benefits along with selling more of your other books?

There's more in the marketing section on how to make your book free if you don't use KDP Select.

KDP also has their Global fund. They put millions of dollars into it every month especially for KDPS authors. How do you get your hands on that money? You know how Amazon Prime members can borrow a book? If they do, you get paid. You know how you can lend an e-book you've bought to someone else via Amazon? If people lend your book, you get paid. With the new Kindle Unlimited program where people sign up for $9.99 a month for as many books as they want? If they download your book, and read at least 10% of it, you get paid.

How much? It depends on how much money Amazon has put into the Global fund that month. The first few months of the Kindle Unlimited program, they put a whole truckload more into the fund and a lot of people made some money.

There are a few other programs for KDPS authors and Amazon is always tweaking and coming up with new ones, so check the KDPS info page to see what's going on right now.

How much money will you make if you sell your e-books through KDP?

Books priced under $2.99 and over $9.99 make 35% royalties. So if your book is $0.99 you'll get about $0.35 for each book. If you aren't signed up for KDPS, some foreign Amazon stores only pay 35% no matter the price. You'll get 70% for books priced $2.99 to $9.99 minus a delivery charge.

When you use the Amazon Countdown promotion, even if you put the book at $0.99 you'll still get 70% royalties.

Amazon pays royalties monthly, but two months after the end of the month in which you sold the book. If you sold books in January, you'll get your money at the end of March.

To make your print books with Amazon you'll use CreateSpace.

They have a lot of resources available to self-publishers including a phone and email helpdesk, a blog, an online community of self-pubbers and professional editing, design, and marketing.

The big decisions when you use CreateSpace are choosing a size of your book, the type of paper to use, whether you want a glossy or matte cover, and which distribution options to choose.

If you're reading the print version of this book, it is 5.5 x 8.5 on cream paper with a matte cover. You can easily have CreateSpace send your proof of the book, but you'll have to pay for it, so make sure it's as good as you can get it before you request that book be sent out to you.

The further your distribution network goes, the more expensive you have to make your book. Keep it reasonable or you won't ever sell any copies. Check your competitive analysis to see how your antecedents are priced.

Release Day

Make time for yourself. This day can be crazy and nerve-jingle-jangling. Release day should be fun, not exhausting.

I suggest having a plan for that day.

There are two parts to a great release day, celebration, and promotion.

There's more information in the marketing section on continuing promotion, but you'll want to do some fun celebration type promotion on release day.

Here are some free promotional things to do on social media.

Post a picture of your book cover and the link to the buy pages for wherever your book is for sale. Write something announcing the release of the book. If you do nothing else on social media today, at least do this one post.

This is the only day I'm allowing you to check your sales rankings a million times, so make it count.

Take a screenshot of the Amazon/B&N/etc. page for your book then post that picture to Facebook or your other social media sites. Write a post saying something like "Yay! My book is finally live on Amazon." #NeverThoughtItWouldHappen

Or "Squee! I'm officially a published author!" #YouKnewMeWhen

You get the idea, something fun and exciting to announce how excited you are that the book is out.

If you're book is doing well in ranking or has hit the top 100 in a category, that's another perfect time to take a screenshot and post that picture too. Say something in your post about how excited you are that the book is being received well and thanks to everyone who's bought it.

It's fun to have a live release day party too. Invite your friends and family to celebrate your release. If they won't buy your book, who will? Have physical copies there to sell and sign. I never give away books to people I expect to buy them.

Break out the party hats and do a celebration at a local book store. Do you have a local independent bookstore? They're always looking for ways to attract new customers. Talk to the owner or manager and see about having a signing and release party there. They might even stalk some of your books.

If there are only chain bookstores that's okay too. The best way to get into their good graces is to bring multiple authors to the game. See if there are any other authors in your area that might want to join you.

If that's a no go, a lot of the bigger chain stores have a coffee shop. Bring a few friends, your party hats, and buy some drinks and coffee from them and have a sort of open house style party. Friends can stop buy anytime while you're there and you can guide people to the website to buy your e-book.

Be sure to take of pictures at whatever kind of party you have, even if it's at home with you and your cats. Then post those pics to your social media accounts too.

Reward yourself.

You're a published author. Su-weet!

I'm serious, this is a huge accomplishment, and you absolutely deserve a reward. Buy yourself the earrings or watch you've been wanting. Go out for a manicure or a massage. Make it a tradition, give yourself a treat every time you publish a book. If you're short on funds, there are plenty of things you can do that don't cost money. Take a long bubble bath with your favorite book and a glass of wine. Sleep in, eat your sack lunch in the park, bake yourself a cake, give yourself time to read a new book or watch a movie you've been meaning to on Netflix. Do something that is going to fill your creativity well back up so you feel great about your accomplishment and can start on the next book.

Too many authors forget about this step in the process. Make it something special.

CHAPTER FIVE

Post publication

Tracking your sales

Congratulations on getting your book out into the world. Now it's time to take care of some business. The first thing you should do is track your sales.

Each of the sales platforms have some sort of report mechanism. Learn them and make friends with them because you'll probably be checking them often.

It's a good idea to keep track of your daily sales as related to your marketing efforts. That way you can see if your efforts are effecting your sales.

There are a few online programs for tracking sales, but most of them just provide you with the same information as your Amazon reports. A few I know of are MetricJunkie, RankForest, and Sales Rank Express. They all have some fun features but I think they are best for tracking a few of your antecedents or 'also boughts' to track how they are doing compared to you.

The one I do like and use is called NovelRank. Again, it only tracks Amazon, but what I like is that you can see your rank in all the different stores in one quick glance. Your rank in each of the stores, like, the UK store, the Canada store, the German store, etc. are all different depending on how many books you've sold there. So you might be selling great in Germany, but not as much in Canada. That can help you figure out where to target some promotions.

There is a free sales tracker spreadsheet on my website at www.coffeebreakpublishing.com that you can use to do that.

When your book initially comes out you'll probably want to monitor those sales very closely, because it's fun to see the money coming in for your efforts for the first time. But if plugging numbers into a spreadsheet everyday seems like a horrible chore you don't have to do it.

It's also nice to track your sales so you can estimate your monthly income. Remember, some sites pay monthly and others quarterly. You should keep track of your sales monthly or at the very least quarterly. It will be important later when you go to pay your taxes. If you're a runaway success and selling thousands of books a month you'll need to look into paying your taxes quarterly. Check with a local tax service, they handle these kinds of things all the time and can guide you through the process.

It's a good idea to keep a file, paper, or on your computer, to keep all your royalty statements from the retailers. Download the reports and keep them. It will help when it comes to tax time.

You can also use them to project future sales. There's more information about creating budgets in The Coffee Break Guide to Business Plans for authors and you can get a budget template for free at www.coffeebreakpublishing.com.

Marketing and Promotion

You need to continue to promote a book every once in a while, even after it's out.

Create an ongoing play and then keep records. Make it flexible so you can do some experimentation for what works for your book, your genre, and your readers.

Keep track of your effort and compare them to your sales so you know what works and what doesn't.

Don't forget about those critical back matter pages. You can change them anytime you feel necessary. If you start a newsletter, put a link in your back matter so people who are reading the book can sign up right then and there. Don't forget to update when you release new books too.

If this is your first book, stick with low cost and free promo. You want to save some of your marketing dollars for when the next and the next books come out. That way when you bring a new reader in they may buy your backlist books too. More books equals more money.

When you have at least ten reviews on Amazon, you can look at doing advertising with email subscription services for readers of e-books. There are a whole bunch of sites that do this, one of the most popular being BookBub. The readers input what kind of books they like to read, usually by genre, and they get emails with books that are on sale or free. The books listed are paid advertisements by the authors or publishers. If you run a sale on your book, this is a great way to let people know. Same goes for free.

Let's talk about free.

Free is a powerful word. Everybody likes getting something for nothing. But do you really want to give away something and get nothing? Why would you use free at all?

Giving away books is a great way to give a whole lot more people a chance to discover you. Hopefully, you'll get some new reviews too. Free books often spur the sale of other books by the same author or in a series. Readers get the first one free and when they like it, go back and buy more. You will probably get some new loyal readers out of the deal. That's powerful. If you've only got one book out, be very careful with free. Use it strategically. Give it away if you're also gaining. If you only have one book available, how is it helping your to make money if you put it for free? You might see your book rise up the free book rankings, and some authors see a slight increase in sales after the free promo because of the increase in visibility, but that's going to drop off fast. You might also get a few more reviews because so many people download your free book. Those are both good, but aren't they even better if you see those benefits along with selling more of your other books?

So how do they do it? Price matching.

You must list your book at other vendors, who allow a $0.00 price point, like Smashwords (and have them distribute to the other retailers like B&N, iBooks and Kobo), first. IBooks let you price at $0.00 directly, so if you've got a Mac you can skip Smashwords. Then report that your book is listed elsewhere at a lower price. You and other customers can report it from your book's page and you should email KDP support and tell them your book can be found at other retailers for a lower price. Amazon only cares about bigger retailers and they still have the prerogative to keep the price as is, if they want.

Making one of your books a loss leader, meaning you give it away for free or super cheap to entice new readers to try your books, is an excellent promotional technique. When you've got three or more books in a series, make that first book free and if it's well written, those readers will come back for more.

Anecdotally, I've heard from several uber-successful self-published authors that their tipping points were when they had a series and put their first book free.

The reader experience

Be aware of your readers' experience. One idea that I've seen a lot of writers use recently is the serialization idea. You release a short story, novella or a portion of a book with a cliffhanger ending. The thought is that the readers are so engaged and really want to know what happens next that they gladly come back and pay for more and more. But, be careful, when done wrong this feels really sleazy to the reader. They feel shorted, nickel and dimed, like they were taken. Why? They didn't know it was going to end that way and now they have to pay more to get the ending they deserve.

I really don't recommend doing this with books you have for sale, and I especially hate it when the first portion is offered for free, with no mention that it is a serial. Just don't do that. However, this can be a lot of fun for you, your readers, and can help you gain potential new readers if you offer the serialization for free on your website or in your newsletter.

Book Giveaways

You can do book giveaways after the book is released too. Goodreads will let you do a giveaway on their site before or after the book is out. Of course, you can do a giveaway on your own site or Facebook whenever you want. Be sure to ask the people who win to let you know how they like the book by giving you a review.

One of my favorite giveaways is the book for a friend. Set up the contest so entrants get to win a book for themselves and one for a friend they think would like it too. You gain new readers and everybody is happy.

Free and easy things to increase sales

There are all kinds of tactics that don't cost a dime and can have great effects on your sales.

Start off with trying different variations of keywords. You usually get about seven words or phrases, but there are probably hundreds of ways to search for your book. Use Google and Amazon to do a few searches to come up with new keywords. Don't change them more than about once a month, but at least three to four times a year. Be sure to keep track of the keywords you've used in case the new ones don't work as well, so you can change them back.

You can do the same thing with categories. When you initially uploaded your book you chose some BISAC categories, and some of those categories, like Fiction/Romance/Contemporary has a truckload of other books. That makes it a lot harder to get to the top of a list.

See if your book fits into a smaller category too. Some retailers don't let the authors choose the smaller niche categories from the self-publishing platform, but sometimes you can get in by emailing the help/support desk. You don't want to switch categories quite as often. Better to climb the charts in one category than have to start at the bottom of one each month. I recommend a category switch only two or three times a year. Once you find the right one, and you'll know when you make it into the top 100, stick with that one as long as you can.

Definitely play around with different price points. Usually, the lower the price, the more books you'll sell. It's all about exposure vs income. Try running a sale, and don't forget to let people know about it. Make sure you track your sales to see which price point does the best for your sales numbers and your income.

Merchandising

Merchandising in the e-book world means the retailers showcase your book. They might feature it somewhere on the website, include it in a newsletter or promotion or include it in a grouping, like say, great beach reads. This is often reserved for the big indie published author or the traditional publishers, but sometimes you can get in on the merchandising opportunities too. The best and easiest way is to email the help/support desk and ask them if your book might fit into any upcoming merchandising, they are creating. Even better if you can suggest a way they could include your book. Did you write a Christmas novella? Great, one less they have to find to include in the Christmas reads merchandising. Especially for holiday opportunities, but also with your new releases, be sure to email them well in advance. They can't do a thing except to say congratulations if you email them the day before your book comes out.

Back Matter

Don't forget about that all important back matter. If you've got more than one book on more than one platform, remember to update the links in your front and back matter and on your website in each of your backlist.

Swag

Be careful with swag items like bookmarks, postcards, trading cards etc. I see too many authors spending hundreds of dollars on these items. They're beautiful junk. Paper gets thrown in the trash and isn't great for getting new readers anyway. Get something cool and use it to reward your loyal readers instead.

Print Books

If you've decided to do a paperback version of your book too, it can be a great promotional tool. I almost always carry a copy of my books with me whenever I'm anywhere readers might be. I've offered tons of free copies to people to read. All I ask is that they give me a review on Amazon.

Don't forget about offline marketing.

One of the best ways I know to get more exposure in real life is appearances. See if you can do a signing at a local bookstore. Give a workshop and make sure to bring your books to sell. My library does a thing called ReadCon every year, and local authors are a big part of the events. Check out book fairs or other library events in your area.

Depending on your genre, there are all kinds of readers' cons for romance, mystery, fantasy and more. Think ComicCon but for romance or mystery novels. They can be expensive for authors, but you get face-to-face time with readers who specifically like books like yours. The ROI (return on investment) is hard to measure for these kind of promotional efforts, but the point here isn't to hand sell a lot of your books, but to let people know about you and what your write.

The marketing section of this book could be a whole book on its own. (If fact, it will be soon!) These are just a few ideas to get you started. Try out a lot of different things, read blogs and articles to get more ideas. My favorite book marketing guru is Penny Sansevieri from Author Marketing Experts. She has free articles and I'm addicted to her newsletter.

For goodness sake, whatever kind of promo and marketing you do, keep track of what you do, when you do it, and how it affects your sales so you know what works and what to do again.

Write the next book

Don't spend so much time promoting one book that you don't write the next one. The best promo is the next book. No really. Write the next book. In fact, I hope you've already started it.

More books sell more books.

It takes about three books to gain a little bit of traction with readers and about ten books to make any real profit.

Yep, ten whole books. And don't think you can cheat by breaking your book up into bits to get to that ten. In fact, it would be great if you could launch a bunch of books all at the same time.

Why? Because if someone reads one of your books and enjoy it, they are likely to come back looking for more. If you don't have more for sale, then you lose out on that additional income.

It used to be that the major authors came out with one book a year. But, if you want to compete in today's high speed, low drag publishing world, you probably need to do more. You start losing favor with the algorithm gods after three to four months. That's when you see sales start to drop. The three month mark is the perfect time to release something new. Yes, that means four books a year. They don't all have to be 100,000 word novels. Readers love to get a glimpse of what characters are doing in between book, so think about some short stories or novellas. If you write non-fiction, think about workbooks that accompany or compliment your book.

If you've got a whole drawer full of books finished that have been sitting under your bed, pull those babies out, polish them up and publish them all!

Don't forget about taxes

I hope you make a truckload of money. But, oh goodness, don't forget to pay your taxes. If you're really going for a career in publishing, and especially self-publishing please, do yourself a favor and talk to a tax professional. Don't wait until March 15th either.

In the USA, if you are making enough money that your taxes would be more than $1000, you need to start paying your taxes quarterly. Yep, Uncle Sam wants his money every three months. And you still have to do that big ole tax return in March. That's the price of success.

How much money equals $1000 worth of taxes? Depends on your tax bracket. But, I'd say when you make your first thousand dollars, go find a tax man (mine's a woman, and she's great, I'm so lucky I found her.)

Although, now that you're running your own small business, (yes, you are), you can also start claiming all kinds of stuff on taxes for deductions, like books.

If you want more information about taking control of your career check out The Coffee Break Guide to Business Plans for Writers. There's a whole section about taxes and about why you really are a small business now.

If you are self-publishing outside of the US, you're going to need an EIN or an ITIN. I have it on good authority that it's much much much easier to get an EIN because you can get one just by phoning the IRS in Philadelphia and asking for one. They'll grill you on a bunch of items and when they are satisfied will fork over the number you need. Without an EIN or ITIN the US retailers will withhold 30% of your revenue until you can prove you're tax exempt (which is what the EIN or ITIN is for.) Don't bother trying to get information from the IRS website on how to obtain these numbers, you'll get mired in the most fabulous of Hotels California. Instead read this brilliant blog by authors Catherine Ryan Howard and David Gaughran at

http://catherineryanhoward.com/2012/02/24/non-us-self-publisher-tax-issues-dont-need-to-be-taxing/

Copyright

I'm not a lawyer, so if you've got literary life and death questions about Intellectual Property (IP) laws and rights, be sure to check with a literary attorney for advice. I am, however, a multi-published author and have spent plenty of time familiarizing myself with my own rights. Here are some things I've learned about copyrights that you might find useful too.

For most of us writers, our work is protected by copyright law the moment we write it down somewhere that is "perceptible either directly or with the aid of a machine or device." That's quote from the Berne Convention for the Protection of Literary and Artistic Works. Most countries in the world are in on this, but there's a few that aren't. If you're in someplace, like say, Inner DingamBoo (where I lived when I first started writing), check for your country's IP laws. They're usually on a government website.

Copyright on your work lasts a long time. You might have heard of the life plus-70 rule. Berne set a minimum duration of a copyright for a literary work equal to the life of the author plus 50 years. Many countries extended that and now the general rule is that a copyright on a literary, dramatic, musical, or artistic work lasts for the life of the author and then until December 31st of the year, 70 years after you die. So, you might want to look into including your copyrights in your will.

For the current list of countries that are signatories to the Berne Convention, visit the World Intellectual Property Organization (WIPO) at www.wipo.int/members/en/

By placing the copyright symbol (©) and a copyright statement in your book, you are telling the world you know your rights, and very importantly giving a legally-relevant date of original publication. That will come in to play if you ever have to sue someone for copyright infringement.

Here's an example of a copyright statement that you could include in your book.

> © 2014, Your Name. Except as provided by the Copyright Act of 1978, no part of this publication may be reproduced, stored in a retrieval system or transmitted in any form or by any means without the prior written permission of the publisher.

The wording for your copyright statement isn't set in stone, so you can use something like this one, or there are a whole slew floating around the Internet you can copy and paste. Find one that you are comfortable with and seems to be traditional for your country.

Usually copyright statements are found in the front of a book, but it's a good idea to put it in the back of your e-book. That way when someone views the preview of your book the copyright page isn't part of that ten percent, and your potential reader gets and actual taste of your work instead of boring legalese.

Putting in a copyright statement is a good start, but if you want all the perks of IP law, you'll probably need to register your copyright. It's a pretty easy process, and for most places you can do it online.

Here are links to a few countries copyright registration systems to get you started:

United States of America

Didn't get enough schoolin' on the law in the 11th grade? You can find the Copyright Act of 1973 at http://copyright.gov/title17/.

US citizens need to officially register with the U.S. Copyright Office before you can make a claim in a US court. The sooner the better, too. Registration may entitle you to statutory damages in a US legal system. The United States Copyright Office website is www.copyright.gov/. It's cheaper and easiest to file online, so look for the Electronic Copyright Office (eCO) and follow the steps at https://eco.copyright.gov/.

It costs $35 for one eCO claim and you can upload the e-book in PDF format right then and there. Be sure to use the single and not the standard form which cost $20 more for no particular reason.

Do yourself a favor and just make it part of the publishing process to pop onto this website and register the same day you publish your book. (Extra special super-secret sneaky tip - register your claim before you publish the print version. That way your e-book is the best possible version available and you don't have to send two copies into the library of congress.)

It is $65, plus the cost to mail everything if you do it the old-fashioned snail mail way. Also, because of heightened security since 9/11 and that anthrax stuff, US Postal service packages are irradiated before they get to the copyright office and if you're sending in paper copies of the book they'll get totally ruined. If you have to submit a print version be sure to send it FedEx, UPS, or DHL instead.

Processing is usually 3-6 months, but it can take up to two years to get your certificate. Expedited service is available when you file your claim, for a flat fee, if you need it to sue the pants off somebody.

Canada

My frozen neighbors to the north can find your copyright law, The Copyright Act (R.S.C, 1985, c. C-42) on the Canadian Intellectual Property Office's website at

http://www.cipo.ic.gc.ca/. There's a link there to register or you can go direct to https://strategis.ic.gc.ca/. A certificate of registration is evidence that your book is protected by copyright and that you are the owner. It can be used in court as evidence of ownership. You can register online and it will cost you $50. The paper and mail version cost $65.

United Kingdom

You Brits, Scots, Welsh, and Northern Irish have the Copyright Act of 1956, The Copyright, Designs and Patents Act of 1988, and Copyright and Related Rights Regulations of 2003. Further information about copyright in the UK can be found at the Intellectual Property Office, at:

http://www.ipo.gov.uk/.

There is no official registration system for copyrighting your books. It is considered an automatic right. (You lucky ducks.)

You can send a copy of any published work to the British Library within one month of publication so that they can include it as part of their records of all published works. Find out more about the British Library and copyright here: http://www.bl.uk/copyright

Australia

Aussie copyright law can be found in the Copyright Act of 1968 (Cth). The Australian Copyright Council has your info and you can find them at:

http://www.ag.gov.au/www/agd/agd.nsf/Page/Copyright.

Copyright is automatic (more lucky ducks) and there is no system in place for "official" registration. You can send a copy of your book to the National Library of Australia. Check with your territory too, because you might need to make a legal deposit to your State library.

New Zealand

The Kiwis have the Copyright Act 1994 and good copyright information can be found from the Copyright Council of New Zealand at http://www.copyright.org.nz/. According to them, no registration is necessary, or even possible, nor is any other formality required for securing copyright protection.

You can send a copy of your new published work to the National Library of New Zealand to be formal proof of the date of your copyright.

CHAPTER SIX

Resources

There are a lot of resources scattered throughout this book, so I thought it might be very nice of me to make you a pretty list with them all here at the back of the book.

Websites

My websites - www.coffeebreakpublishing.com
www.coffeebreaksocialmedia.com
Peanut   butter   on   the   keyboard   –
www.peanutbutteronthekeyboard.com
NaNoWriMo – www.nanowrimo.com
LitLift - www.litlift.com/
Writer Beware - http://accrispin.blogspot.com/
Predators and Editors - http://pred-ed.com/
The Book Designer - www.thebookdesigner.com/
A   Newbie's   Guide   to   Self-Publishing   -
http://jakonrath.blogspot.com/

Business and Taxes

http://www.irs.gov/uac/Is-Your-Hobby-a-For-Profit-Endeavor%3F

http://catherineryanhoward.com/2012/02/24/non-us-self-publisher-tax-issues-dont-need-to-be-taxing/

Writers Organizations

Romance Writers of America – www.rwa.org

Sisters in Crime - www.sistersincrime.org/

Science Fiction and Fantasy Writers of America - www.sfwa.org

American Society of Journalists and Authors - www.asja.org/

Society of Children's Book Writers and Illustrators - www.scbwi.org/

Alliance of Independent Authors - allianceindependentauthors.org/

Novelists, Inc. - www.ninc.com/

Books

Coffee Break Guide to Social Media for Writers by Amy Denim

Coffee Break Guide to Business Plans for Writers by Amy Denim

Author, Publisher, Entrepreneur by Guy Kawasaki

How to Sell Books by the Truckload on Amazon by Penny Sansevieri

Smashwords Style Guide by Mark Coker

Workshops

Before You Hit Send with Angela James - http://nicemommy-evileditor.com/before-you-hit-send/

Lawson Writers Academy - www.margielawson.com/lawson-writers-academy-courses

Candace Haven's Fast Draft - www.candacehavens.com/index.php/workshops/

Agents

www.AgentQuery.com.

Writer's Digest guide to literary agents - http://www.writersdigest.com/editor-blogs/guide-to-literary-agents

Money

Brenda Hiatt's Show Me the Money report - http://brendahiatt.com/show-me-the-money/indie-earnings/

Writing and Editing

Dragon - www.nuance.com/dragon/index.htm

Freedom - https://macfreedom.com/

Open Office - https://www.openoffice.org/

Scrivener - www.literatureandlatte.com

ZenWriter - http://zenwriter.tumblr.com/ and http://www.beenokle.com/zenwriter.html

Writer's Cafe - www.writerscafe.co.uk/

Storyist - http://storyist.com

Page Four and Smart Edit - http://www.softwareforwriting.com/

Ywriter - www.spacejock.com/yWriter5.html

Plume Creator - www.plume-creator.eu/

Focus Writer - http://gottcode.org/focuswriter/

LitLift - http://www.litlift.com/

OneNote - www.onenote.com/

Evernote - www.evernote.com/

Name Dice - http://thinkamingo.com/name-dice/

Critique Partners and Beta Readers

Ladies Who Critique http://www.ladieswhocritique.com

How About We CP http://howaboutwecp.tumblr.com/

Critique Circle http://www.critiquecircle.com/Default.asp

CP Seek http://www.cpseek.com/index.php.

World Literary Cafe –
http://www.worldliterarycafe.com/forum/125

Serenity Editor - http://www.serenity-software.com/

Style Writer - http://www.stylewriter-usa.com/stylewriter-free-download.php

Writer's Digest - http://www.writersdigestshop.com/author-service-center/editing-service

---

Places to back up your files

Drop Box - www.dropbox.com

SugarSync - www.sugarsync.com

OneDrive - https://onedrive.live.com/

iCloud - www.icloud.com/

Google Drive - https://drive.google.com/

Social Media and Websites

Word Press - http://www.wordpress.com or www.wordpress.org

Facebook – www.facebook.com

Twitter – www.twitter.com

Goodreads – www.goodreads.com

Book Retailers, Distributors, and Aggregators

Amazon KDP - http://www.kdp.amazon.com and forums.kindledirectpublishing.com

Amazon CreateSpace - www.createspace.com

Amazon ACX - www.acx.com

Apple iBooks - https://www.apple.com/ibooks-author/ and https://itunesconnect.apple.com/WebObjects/iTunesConnect.woa/wa/bookSignup

Barnes & Noble, Nook Press - www.nookpress.com

Kobo Writing Life - www.writinglife.kobobooks.com

Google Play Books - https://play.google.com/books/publish

Books-a-Million (BAM) - http://www.diy.bampublish.com and http://bampublish.com/publishing-services.html

OmniLit & AllRomance eBooks – https://www.allromanceebooks.com/publisherRegistration.html

Smashwords - www.smashwords.com

Draft 2 Digital - https://www.draft2digital.com/

XinXii - http://www.xinxii.com/publish.php

IngramSpark - https://www1.ingramspark.com/

Lulu - http://www.lulu.com/create/books/

Bookbaby - http://www.bookbaby.com/

Book Formatting

Amazon's list of HTML –
https://kdp.amazon.com/help?topicId=A377RPHW6ZG4D8.
Book Design Templates - www.bookdesigntemplates.com
Marie Force's Formatting Fairies –
http://e-bookformattingfairies.blogspot.com/
or https://marieforce.com/formatting-fairies
BB eBooks - http://bbebooksthailand.com/
Adobe InDesign –
 http://www.adobe.com/products/indesign.html
Jutoh - http://www.jutoh.com/
Scrivener - www.literatureandlatte.com
Calibre - http://calibre-ebook.com/
Sigil –
http://download.cnet.com/Sigil/3000-2351_4-75332057.html
Epub Validator - http://validator.idpf.org/

ISBN information

Bowker - http://www.bowker.com or www.myidentifiers.com
Canadian ISBNs - http://www.collectionscanada.gc.ca/ciss-ssci/index-e.html
UK ISBNs –
http://www.isbn.nielsenbook.co.uk/uploads/BookNet_OnlineOrderCollectionService_Sept13(1).pdf
Australian ISBNs - https://www.myidentifiers.com.au/
New Zealand ISBNs - http://natlib.govt.nz/forms/isn

Tracking your sales

Free spreadsheet at www.coffeebreakpublishing.com/books

NovelRank - www.novelrank.com

Book Promotion and Marketing

BookBub - https://www.bookbub.com/partners

ENT - http://ereadernewstoday.com/bargain-and-free-book-submissions/

Goodreads - https://www.goodreads.com/advertisers

Author Marketing Experts –

http://www.amarketingexpert.com/about-ame/penny-sansevieri/

Copyrights

USA –

http://copyright.gov/title17/ and http://www.copyright.gov/ and

https://eco.copyright.gov/eService_enu/start.swe?SWECmd=Start&SWEHo=eco.copyright.gov

Canada –

http://www.cipo.ic.gc.ca/eic/site/cipointernet-internetopic.nsf/eng/h_wr00003.html

https://strategis.ic.gc.ca/app/scr/opic-cipo/da-cpr/depot-filing/connexion-login_eng.htm?wt_src=cipo-cpyrght-main&wt_cxt=toptask

UK –

http://www.ipo.gov.uk/types/copy.htm

and http://www.bl.uk/copyright

Australia –
http://www.ag.gov.au/www/agd/agd.nsf/Page/Copyright

New Zealand - http://www.copyright.org.nz/

The Coffee Break Guide to Social Media for Writers

HOW TO SUCCEED ON SOCIAL MEDIA AND STILL HAVE TIME TO WRITE

CHAPTER 1

The Social Media Monster

Don't Let Social Media Scare You

When I first got serious about writing, I joined a local writing group. Best idea I ever had. They've given me so much support from day one. I highly recommend this step for anyone who wants to make a go at writing and selling his or her work.

One of the first events my group put on after I joined was a writers' retreat. We went up to the mountains, got all inspired by the wildlife, the scenery, and the hot tub. There may also have been some wine involved. Good times.

We spent a chunk of the weekend putting words on the page. But, we also had a few guest speakers to boost our morale and inspire our writing. One of our presenters was an editor from a small, but growing, press. Her topic was query letters, but as writers and editors tend to do, we moved off like a rocket on a tangent.

Social media.

And it scared the living nightlife out of me.

She threw around words like platform, followers, tweet, and discoverability. This big bad scary editor said I should have my platform established two years before I submitted anything. Ahhhh!

I didn't even know what a platform was, much less how to create one online. I wasn't on Twitter, I'd never heard of Goodreads, Pinterest was just a funny word, and the only time I spent on Facebook was to take weird surveys, play farming games, and tag pictures of my drunken friends.

But, if I wanted to be a published author, it seemed I needed to do more than just write. Who knew?

This relaxing weekend in the mountains left me in need of some meditation and a massage. But I skipped the yoga and went out and bought a smartphone instead.

I spent the next year becoming a social media fiend. And I barely finished one manuscript. I had created an online presence, but I had diddly-squat to pitch. Oops.

The purpose of writing this book is, A: To help all those authors out there who've been scared by social media create their own online platform, and 2: Give them time to actually write.

Novel concept. I know.

Social media doesn't have to be scary. You can use social media effectively (it's really not as scary as some people I know make it out to be) and still have time to write. Social media can be your friend. I'll get you an introduction.

Author, this is Social Media. No, wait come back here. I promise it's not the big, scary, mean, time-sucking monster it looks like. Breathe. Okay, good. Let's try again. Author, this is Social Media. Yes, you can shake hands, it won't bite.

Good job.

Social Media, this is Author. You're going to become good friends.

Any time this all becomes too much, come back to this page, breathe, and read the tips again.

Social media is your friend. It doesn't have to take away from the time you spend doing what you love. Five quality minutes a day is all you really need. Thirty quality minutes spread throughout the day will do wonders.

Coffee Break Social Media Tips

Be present. Don't post and run. Do take on social media when you will be available to interact should someone respond to you—on any of your platforms. The key is to be social and interactive. Not a robot.

Use a ten-to-one ratio for marketing yourself or your books. For every ten social interactions you can have one, just one self-promo. People don't like, or buy spam.

As you get into your platforms and your breaks, you'll learn what you do and don't like to do. DO what you like.

Don't let social media overwhelm you. If you're jumping between platforms and spending more time on social media than on what you love to do, scale it back. Start back at the beginning and just concentrate on your primary platform. Ease yourself into other platforms when you are good and ready.

The Best Platform is the Next Book

You can spend all day, every day, building your platform on social media, but if you don't actually write a book, it won't do you a bit of good. Establishing your platform and using social media is always time spent not writing your book. Without a book, there's nothing for you to establish a platform for. So, get your butt in the chair and write that book. And when you finish that one, write the next one, and the next one. A good quality story will sell you, your brand, and your books better than any website, Facebook post, or tweet.

How This Book Works

In the next chapter, I'll introduce you to the Coffee Break Mentality. It's the key. Social media is there to give you a boost, but it shouldn't take away from your writing time. The coffee break strategies in this book should help you figure out how to be on social media and still have time to write.

You don't have to read every chapter. After you get those key concepts, you can flip through the next few chapters to check out the writer's best social media sites. There's a chapter on your website and blogging, Facebook, Twitter, Pinterest, and Goodreads. For each, there are details on what you need to do once, every once in a while, what to do once you've got your groove on, and what to do on your social media breaks.

There are so many great social media networks these days that this would be a four-billion-page book if there were a chapter on each of them. Instead, included is a chapter with twelve additional networks with briefs on how to use them. There is also a chapter on Social Media tools, websites, and services to help you get the most out of your social media efforts.

At the end of the book, there is an example social media plan, and templates for you to create your own social media plan.

In case I go too techy-fancy-schmancy on you, there is a glossary at the end of the book where you can get simply worded definitions for some of the terms I use.

For example: Platform — noun, a place where you represent yourself and your writing to the world in order to gain more fans. Examples: your website, your Facebook page, your Twitter account, personal appearances, your books, etc.

One Teeny Tiny Final Note

This book will be out of date the moment it's published. It's simply the nature of social media (or today's world, really). This book will have to be updated, and I'll do that, as well as post updates on my website www.coffeebreaksocialmedia.com. But know going in, that something in these pages will be wrong, out of date, or simply not exist anymore when you read this. You'll have to do some research on your own sometimes. It's okay. Google will help you.

Let's get started.

If you enjoyed this excerpt and want to read more of The Coffee Break Guide to Social Media for Writers, you can get it on Amazon.

A Thank You from the Author

Dear Reader (who is probably also a writer),

Before you are off to read your next book I wanted to take a quick moment to say thank you for reading this one.

When you go shopping for books to help improve your writing life they are often on the writing craft, but you chose another direction and took a chance on learning about self-publishing with me. I appreciate that you downloaded and read this book all the way to the end (where you are now).

Remember there are a lot of great, free downloadable resources just for readers of this book. If you missed clicking on the links in any chapter, the templates can all be accessed at

www.coffeebreakpublishing.com/books/resources.

We all know reviews are the king of word-of-mouth marketing. I would be eternally grateful if you would spread the word about The Coffee Break Guide to Self Publishing. It will help me understand what you liked, what was useful, and to write more business books for authors like you.

Would you take a minute to leave a review for this book? Amazon, Goodreads, or anywhere else you like to discuss books.

If your writer friends out there in the social-media-o-sphere might like (or need) this book to help them focus their writing life like you have, please let them know about it. You can get me at:

@AmyDenim on Twitter

Facebook: www.facebook.com/AuthorAmyDenim

If you liked the content and found the information here useful please let me know. If you have corrections or suggestions for the next version, get those to me too. I love to hear from readers and writers.

Best wishes,

~Amy

ABOUT THE AUTHOR

Amy Denim writes business books for writers and contemporary romance. She loves hot heroes (like chefs and cowboys) and curvy intelligent heroines (like chefs and cowgirls.)

She's been a franchise sales coordinator, a lifeguard, a personal shopper, and a teacher of English as a Foreign Language. But now she spends her days reading and writing at her local library or in her book cave.

Amy started out her writer's life scared out of her wits because she didn't have a business plan, hadn't yet created an online platform, wasn't on twitter, didn't have a Facebook fanpage and had never even heard of Goodreads. She just wrote books. So she spent a year becoming a publishing industry information fiend and now does consulting for creatives on how to use take control of their writing careers. She started Coffee Break Social Media to help writers and artists learn to use SM platforms effectively (without the scare tactics) but still have time to create. She believes business plans and social media can be every writer's friend, sometimes they just need an introduction.

Visit Amy on her author website at www.AmyDenim.com or for tips and tricks on the writing business at

www.coffeebreaksocialmedia.com.